Coping with

REJECTION

Barbara Moe

The Rosen Publishing Group, Inc.
New York

Published in 2001 by The Rosen Publishing Group, Inc.
29 East 21st Street, New York, NY 10010

Copyright © 2001 by Barbara Moe

First Edition

Cover Photo © Digital Vision

Library of Congress Cataloging-in-Publication Data

Moe, Barbara.
Coping with rejection / by Barbara Moe. — 1st ed.
p. cm. — (Coping with)
Includes bibliographical references and index.
ISBN: 978-1-4358-8710-7
1. Rejection (Psychology) in adolescence—Juvenile literature.
[1. Rejection (Psychology) 2. Emotions. 3. Interpersonal relations.]
I. Title. II. Coping.
BF724.3.R44 M64 2001
158.2—dc21

                                        2001000459

Manufactured in the United States of America

Contents

Introduction

Sara tries to participate in an ongoing conversation between her friends Becky and Crystal. But Becky and Crystal continue talking, leaving Sara out. Sara wonders what she did to deserve this rejection.

Ben returns a pair of ripped shorts to the store. He bought them the day before and didn't notice the rip until he got home. The salesperson treats him like a criminal. What's wrong with this picture, Ben wonders. It's not as if he stole this defective merchandise. Rejection!

Jake's computer crashes just as he gets ready to stay up all night writing his final English paper. Why is this stupid machine rejecting him just when he needs its services most?

Rejection. It's a mean-sounding word. The dictionary gives the verb "reject" some downbeat definitions, including:

➥ The refusal to accept or admit someone.

➥ The refusal to grant a request or demand.

➥ The discarding of something useless or unsatisfactory ("We don't need you").

The noun "reject" (as in "You're just a reject on the scrap heap of life") is a person or thing tossed away as unnecessary,

1

unwanted, or imperfect. It's important to keep in mind that getting rejected does not mean that you are a reject.

No one escapes rejection. Even if your mom and dad could protect you from rejection, they won't be on the field when the coach announces that all of your friends made varsity soccer and you didn't. They won't be standing beside you when you get turned down for the fifth summer job you've applied for.

Mini-rejections can ruin your day. Major rejections can turn you into a bitter person, someone who withdraws from life and its challenges. In this book, you will learn that you can't avoid rejection, but you can learn to live with it in healthy ways. You'll also learn:

- In what areas of life rejection occurs

- How rejection stirs up old hurts and losses

- How to identify and deal with the common feelings that accompany rejection

- How to heal yourself by practicing forgiveness

- How not to take rejection personally

- How to take care of yourself and make positive changes in your life

- How to overcome the fear of rejection and dare to take healthy risks

There is no single right way to deal with rejection. Do what you think will work best for you.

Rejection: That's Life!

Before we look at all of the areas of life in which we experience rejection, let's consider the way we live.

People in the Western world have many wants. We want a new computer, the latest in stereo equipment, a large bank account, and more. As soon as we get all of the things we thought we wanted, we start wanting more.

We desire fame and fortune. If we fall short, we feel rejected, unimportant, even worthless. We claw and grasp our way to the top—wherever that is. Eastern philosophies such as Buddhism de-emphasize striving and emphasize being and living in the present. But even if we tone down our want list, we cannot totally avoid rejection. It happens so fast—a frown, a cold shoulder, a cutting remark.

Bam! The insult hurts some people more than others. Why? Why does the same intensity of rejection barely faze one person while knocking the socks off another? Why can one person shake off rejection while another broods for days, weeks, months, or even years?

Our Heritage

One theory is that some people are born more sensitive than others. Sensitivity is a useful quality; it keeps us from

3

hurting others. But heightened sensitivity may make us more vulnerable to rejection. There is nothing we can do to change our genetic makeup, but we can be aware of it.

Family Rejection

Another theory is that early childhood rejection makes people more likely to feel the sting of rejection when they get older. If newborn infants could talk, they might tell us they felt rejected from the moment of birth. Their mothers' bodies protected them for nine months until they were thrust into the cruel world.

Chances are that when you were an infant, your parents looked at you, so tiny and defenseless, and vowed to protect you from all hurt and harm. But they couldn't. No matter how loving your parents were, they couldn't give you everything.

Lisa's mom carries around a lot of guilt about her mothering. "When I had you," she says, "I was not very grown up at all. After your birth, we moved to Manhattan, where we didn't know a soul. Your dad started a new job, he was hardly ever home, and you had colic."

"What's colic?" asks Lisa.

"Sort of like gas pains," says her mom. "You cried and cried. Nothing I did comforted you. I felt helpless and angry. So I put you in your crib and let you cry yourself to sleep."

Although Lisa can imagine her mother's frustration, it wasn't Lisa's fault that she had gas pains. Just hearing the story makes her feel rejected.

4

On the other hand, it's not hard to see that even loving parents sometimes have to say no to their children. ("No, dear, you cannot cross the highway on your tricycle." Or "I'm sorry, honey, but you can't have three chocolate bars for breakfast.")

For any child, learning to deal with rejection starts early. But many parents are not aware of a child's feelings. Even if they do understand, they may not know how to help. Below are three parental reactions to a child's feelings caused by rejection. Which would have felt most comforting to you?

Child (crying): "Lexie and Carlene won't let me play with them!"

Parent (fuming): "What? Those brats. I'm going to call their mothers."

Parent (sighing): "You probably did something to annoy them. You need to work on your behavior."

Parent (holding out his or her arms): "I bet you feel sad and left out. Come here and I'll give you a hug."

Rejection from parents and from other family members is often unintentional. Busy adults are trying to meet their own needs, as well as yours, and may not have much energy left over. Sometimes they make thoughtless remarks.

"Here's how it was in my house," says Sam. "My parents went by the old traditions. My dad went off to work every day, and Mom took care of the house and kids. When Dad came home, he went straight to his easy chair and stuck his head in the newspaper. Mom had been home all day with us; she wanted some

attention from him. We wanted attention from him, too, but he was tired. He'd fall asleep behind his paper. I didn't realize it at the time, but now I think that my dad's so-called rejection in the past has made me more sensitive to rejection today."

Carrie's parents sent her first-grade school photos to some of their relatives. Aunt Ida wrote back to Carrie. "Thanks for the photo," she said. "I bet when your teeth come in, you're going to have a pretty smile." Carrie still remembers how proud she felt at being able to read Aunt Ida's printing but how upset she felt about the comment. Did Aunt Ida mean she didn't have a pretty smile now? Did Aunt Ida like her less because of her "ugly" smile?

Shaunda's aunt and uncle were in the kitchen eating ice cream and talking to her parents when eight-year-old Shaunda came in with her best friend, Jackie. "Could we have some ice cream, too?" Shaunda asked.
"Sure," said her dad. "Help yourselves."
As Shaunda stood at the freezer, she heard Aunt Lucy's comment. "Aren't they cute together? One so skinny and the other one so chubby you'd just like to pinch her." Suddenly Shaunda didn't want any ice cream. She wanted to melt away. Aunt Lucy hadn't mentioned any names, but Shaunda knew she wasn't the skinny one.

Degrees of Rejection

Rejection can vary in degree from mild to severe. A crusty look from a stranger would be on the low-impact end of the scale. The breakup of a long-term relationship would be somewhere in the middle. Abandonment by or loss of a parent is on the highest-impact end.

Abandonment and Abuse

Abandonment by a parent is one of the most powerful kinds of rejection that can happen to a child. Some children also experience neglect, or physical, sexual, or emotional abuse. Each experience causes further damage to a child's sense of self. When children have experienced this degree of rejection, they may begin to reject themselves. They may think of themselves as flawed.

Greg felt that his mother had rejected him before birth. She wasn't married to Greg's father. Greg lived with his mother for a while, then with his grandmother, and then back with his mother and her boyfriend. Meanwhile, his behavior became hard to handle. When Greg was seven years old, his mother took him to the local social services department and left him there. By this time, several of her boyfriends had abused him.

Greg's social workers found him an adoptive home with a couple with three older children. Greg expected this family to reject him just as his birthmother had done. He decided he might as well make the rejection happen sooner rather than later. He refused to do chores, stole money from various family members, stole money from kids and teachers at school, broke into neighbors' houses and stole from them, and shoplifted from the local convenience store. He got into fights with friends, making sure they rejected him, too.

His adoptive parents tried several therapists. One of them told the parents that Greg was damaged goods

7

and there was nothing he could do to help. At the time, Greg wasn't interested in therapy anyway.

When Greg turned eighteen, his parents asked him to move out and live on his own. Greg did not want to go. His parents insisted, making Greg feel rejected again. He spent some time in jail and some time living on the streets. Now, at age nineteen, Greg is beginning to realize how his early experiences made him sensitive to rejection. He has decided to get counseling.

Death of a Parent

Calling death a rejection may seem like a stretch. In most cases, the parent did not want to die. But the death of a parent may feel like rejection to the young child left behind. In her book, *The Loss That Is Forever: The Lifelong Impact of the Early Death of a Mother or Father*, Maxine Harris says that a parent's death causes a child to be "at a loss for words" in every sense.

Emily is a grandmother now. But she remembers exactly where in the living room she stood, by the bookcase, when her mother squeezed her hands and said, "Your dad is very sick, and I need your help."

Emily nodded and hugged her mom. "I'll help, Mom." An only child, she prayed every day that God would heal her beloved father. She tried to be a good girl for the sake of her mother.

But three years later, Emily's father died. Although he did not commit suicide, Emily felt rejected, not only by her father but also by God. How could her father leave her? How could God have let her father die? Didn't God answer prayers? Hadn't she been good enough?

When Emily had her first child, she thought: What if something happens to him? What if he gets a terrible disease? She wonders now if in some ways she withdrew from her son to protect herself from getting hurt.

The flood of feelings is even greater if the parental death is a suicide. Harris says young children almost always believe that their parents love them. Until a child gets some insight into the parent's state of mind at the time, a suicide may feel like the ultimate rejection.

The Impact of Divorce

Parental divorce can also cause a child to feel rejected.

Bob's parents divorced and his father left the family when Bob was eight years old. At first, Bob and his brother saw their father regularly. Over time, however, they saw less of him, until eventually contact stopped. Bob tried to pretend that the divorce had not affected him. But he realized later that his mom, working hard to support two children alone, could not be as involved in his life as he wished. He still feels sad when he remembers that his parents never attended his school events.

Handicaps

Another type of parental rejection occurs when a child is born with a handicap that a parent has trouble accepting.

Claire was born with impaired vision. Friends of the young parents made "helpful" suggestions. Some said Claire's parents should make an adoption plan for their baby daughter. Others suggested they send

9

Claire to a residential school for the blind as soon as possible. Claire's parents did neither. They raised their daughter to be a self-sufficient adult. Claire recently graduated from college and has her first teaching job with twenty-three second graders. Claire has heard from several relatives that although her father turned out to be a kind and attentive parent, there was a period during which he was so upset, he withdrew from Claire and didn't even hold her.

Relationships

One of the most common places for rejection is in relationships, both same sex and opposite sex. The example below shows how rejection affected two girls who were friends.

Lisa (the colicky baby of the earlier story) had become friends with Sierra. They didn't do much together outside school, but they did share some of the same classes. One day after school, Sierra surprised Lisa by saying, "I'm having a lot of trouble at home. My mom is a total witch. Do you think I could come live at your house for a while until I find another place?"

Lisa hesitated. She liked to help people, and she knew her parents did, too. But her mom had just had surgery for cancer and was having chemotherapy. Her dad had recently lost his job.

"I'm not sure," Lisa said. "I'll ask my parents and let you know tomorrow." That night Lisa had trouble sleeping. She decided not to ask her parents.

The next day Sierra stopped Lisa in the hall. "What did they say?"

"Actually . . . um . . . it won't work right now," said Lisa. "We have too much going on."

"That's okay," said Sierra. "Thanks for asking."

Lisa could tell by the way Sierra turned and walked away that her friend felt angry and rejected. Lisa felt sad; she had let her friend down. She hoped their friendship would survive.

Sierra and Lisa never again discussed Sierra's problems at home. Lisa noticed that although Sierra seemed superficially friendly, she talked to her less and less. A few weeks later, Sierra moved in with a girl named Erin, and Lisa's friendship with Sierra faded away.

The rejection hurt, and Lisa couldn't stop thinking about it. She wondered if her experience as a baby with colic, crying and crying, lonely in her crib, had made her more sensitive than normal to rejection. Lisa was smart enough to know that both she and Sierra had felt rejected.

Many people could fill a book with opposite-sex rejection stories. The dating scene calls for a strange kind of commitment. After more than one date, a guy and a girl are considered a couple. This relationship is usually followed at some time by a breakup in which at least one of the parties feels rejected.

Jessica says, "He was the love of my life—or so I thought. I was eighteen and he was twenty-three, sexy and rebellious. He left notes on my car and called me 'Sunshine.' We even talked about someday having kids together.

"But it's amazing the relationship lasted as long as it did. Tom's idea of a compliment went something like this: 'You know what? You have great childbearing hips.' Ugh. I think I was a challenge to him because I called him on negative behaviors and his habit of escaping problems by using alcohol and drugs.

"One morning after a year of dating, he told me he wanted to break up with me. I don't even remember what he said. But I do remember coming home and running into the bathroom to cry. After a few minutes, I looked into the mirror and said to my red, swollen face, 'Jessica, you are better off without him.'"

Other places where rejection commonly occurs are schools, camps, or other structured settings.

Remember Emily, whose father died when she was young? Emily's mother poured all of her resources into her daughter. Emily took violin, piano, and dance lessons. Although Emily wanted to be an actress, her mother did not want to expose Emily to rejection. She encouraged her daughter to excel in music, and Emily did not disappoint her. In the summer between her sophomore and junior years in high school, Emily attended a summer arts camp. Some of the young virtuosos practiced their instruments for several hours every day, but Emily preferred to socialize. For some reason, the orchestra conductor took an intense dislike to her. For the final concert, the one to which all of her relatives were invited, the conductor gave Emily the last chair. In addition, he asked her not to play at all during the second half of the concert.

"I shouldn't have taken it so hard," says Emily years later. "Maybe my early experiences with rejection made me overly sensitive. Although I still played the violin, my heart wasn't in it. But maybe some good came from that horrible experience. I'm a junior high school teacher now, and I'm very tuned into my students' experiences with rejection."

Jobs

Getting fired (or never hired), especially for those new to the job market, can feel like total rejection.

What Steve likes to call his first job-hunting fiasco occurred the summer he turned sixteen. He'd never applied for a job before and wasn't looking forward to the experience. However, his parents had gotten on his case. They must have thought he was going to turn into a bum.

One day about 2 PM, Steve took the bus downtown. He walked into a Greek restaurant, where two young men sat smoking after the lunch rush. "I'd like to apply for a job," said Steve. His hand was shaking around the pen he'd brought along to fill out the application.

At first neither of the men said anything. During the long pause, Steve broke out in a sweat. Finally, the two guys looked at each other and started laughing.

As he turned and rushed out of the restaurant, Steve wasn't laughing. Tears stung his eyes. Did he look funny? Had he said something wrong? Steve made no more job applications that day. He got on the next bus and went home.

Getting fired from a paying job is a definite rejection, but people also end up feeling rejected even in jobs they do for fun.

When It's Not Your Fault

Even more difficult to understand than individual rejections are those that occur because of the ways other people choose to categorize us—by race/ethnicity, social/financial status, sexual orientation, religion, or disability, to name a few. Often, whichever group is in the majority rejects those of the minority. Almost everyone wants to stand out from the group and be unique, while at the same time, people want to fit in and be like everyone else.

Although religious tolerance is one foundation on which our society is based, young people may reject others because of religious differences. A group of teens makes fun of a Muslim woman because her face is covered; a person points and laughs at a Jewish boy's yarmulke.

Almost everyone has some kind of imperfection—a big nose, nearsighted eyes, too much weight or not enough. But those with the most severe disabilities—blindness, deafness, paralysis, or missing limbs—seem to suffer the most from rejection.

Much of the problem is that "normal" people don't know how to act around the "handicapped" person. Does the person in the wheelchair want a push? Does the blind person want help crossing the street? Many people with handicapping conditions are fiercely independent. They would rather have your friendship than your "help." If you ask, they are often happy to tell you what they need—or don't need. If you don't ask and your help is rejected, you may end up feeling rejected.

There are many reasons for the rejection of people with disabilities. Subconsciously, people fear that they, too, could end up deaf or paralyzed; being around someone

14

with such a handicap reminds them of their vulnerability. Or they may fear rejection themselves because of their association with a handicapped person. Most young people worry about fitting in. Many of those with a disability don't get a chance to fit in.

Experts say that one in ten people is gay. That puts those who are homosexual in the minority. In general, society rejects same-sex relationships. Even if parents accept a young gay couple, peers may not. Or people of the same age may accept the relationship, while those of the older generation do not.

Although these rejections have nothing to do with us as people, they still have the power to hurt us—if we let them.

Ron was sixteen when he went to live with his mother on an Indian reservation in Arizona. Ron's mother taught school, and Ron attended a high school in which he was the only non–Native American. Here Ron experienced for the first time the kind of rejection other minorities often feel. Never before in his life had Ron felt so left out. The other guys teased him, laughed at him, and bullied him. One person, however, befriended him. Not only did Dalton try to protect Ron, he gave him a horse to ride. Ron never forgot Dalton's kindness, which changed his view of the reservation and began his lifelong interest in horses.

As author Marlene Fay Watson points out, racism even exists within families. Watson observes that within her own family and others, including African American, Latino, and Asian, those with lighter skin may reject those who have darker skin. "We ended up believing . . . lighter is more desirable, lighter is more successful, lighter is the ticket out of poverty."

Rejection can cause people to dislike themselves. When Watson visited her ninety-three-year-old grandmother in a nursing home, her grandmother remembered the pain of rejection by her own family and others. Her sister, she said, the one with the lighter skin, was the "pretty one."

Social/Financial Status

We've all heard the expression "Money talks." We've also heard the expression "Money can't buy happiness." In real life, both may be true.

Paul feels rejected because most of the kids he has grown up with go to soccer camp every summer. His parents tell him they can't afford to send him.

Angel feels rejected because the dress she's wearing to the prom came from the "slightly used" store and looks dorky.

Ed feels rejected because his single mother is a produce manager at a supermarket; most of his friends (or the people he would like to be friends with) have parents who are accountants, engineers, doctors, or lawyers.

People have various reasons for rejecting those with less money than they have. Money and social status make certain people feel important. Some people can accept themselves only if they are rich and own lots of things.

Deal with
How You Feel

Here is a summary of common postrejection reactions:

↪ Numbness, shock, denial

↪ Anger, rage, the desire for revenge

↪ Embarrassment, humiliation, shame

↪ Depression, self-blame

↪ A need for action to relieve the feelings

You may have only one of these reactions, you may have one after another, or you may have all of them at once in a great big overwhelming jumble.

Say you get a toothache. Your first reaction might be to ignore it and hope the pain will go away. ("I shouldn't have chewed up that jawbreaker yesterday.") Your second reaction could be anger. ("Why does the government allow stores to sell those dangerous pieces of candy that ruin people's teeth?") Next you might feel embarrassed. ("Four-year-olds try to chew up jawbreakers, but sixteen-year-olds should know better.") You might react with self-blame and depression. ("If I can hurt myself doing a simple thing like chewing, I better stay in bed today.") Almost any emotion is possible. If you are already feeling down, a broken tooth could be the last straw. For example, "Yesterday I lost my glasses, this morning I fought with my girlfriend, and this afternoon I'm on my way to the dentist."

Positive action can cause you to become a stronger person. Negative action can cause almost unbelievable destruction. In the essay "The Classroom Avenger," Baltimore police psychologist James McGee writes about lifestyles and personality traits characteristic of the seventeen teenagers who killed forty-five students and teachers (and wounded eighty-five others) in school murders, beginning in 1993 and ending after fifteen people were killed at Columbine High School in Littleton, Colorado, in 1999. According to the study, all of the killers considered themselves social outcasts who had suffered from teasing and victimization by educators and other students. They were all overly sensitive to criticism or rejection and had found the most negative way imaginable to deal with their feelings.

Brandon had completed an intense application process for his dream summer job at the Nature and Science Museum, a short bike ride from his house. He had zipped through his first and second interviews. The job involved pushing a cart around the museum. The cart held various specimens, such as fossils, and a magnifying glass that kids could use for inspection.

All of the people he met during the interviewing process were friendly and encouraging. On his first day of work, however, Brandon had a brief orientation from his supervisor, the sour-faced son of the museum director.

18

Brandon, who considered himself someone who could get along with most people, tried to like Arthur. But on the second day, when a group of employees went out to lunch, Brandon made the apparent mistake of calling his supervisor "Art" as others had done. Arthur immediately turned his glare on Brandon. "It's Arthur to you, son—or better yet, you can call me Mr. Cavanaugh."

Brandon felt the slap of this put-down; his face burned and his heart pounded.

In the days that followed, things went quickly downhill. "Mr. Cavanaugh" accused him of coming in late, taking long breaks, and talking too much to other staff. None of these accusations were true. Nevertheless, a week after being hired, Brandon got fired.

Brandon's initial reaction to this rejection was no feeling at all. He got on his bike and took off for home. Later, he realized he didn't remember the ride home; he had put himself on automatic pilot.

After the numbness came denial. "It makes no difference to me," Brandon said. "There are hundreds of other jobs out there. I didn't want to work at that old museum anyway."

By the afternoon, Brandon's anger had surfaced. When people can't talk about their angry feelings, they may act them out—either accidentally or on purpose. That evening, Brandon slammed a closet door on his finger and kicked the dog.

People acting out their anger sometimes pick fights with innocent people or try to numb their anger by smoking, drinking, using drugs, gambling, reckless driving, or compulsive spending.

Later, Brandon told himself he would never go near the museum again; he couldn't stand to look at the place. Anger turned into a desire for revenge; he thought of throwing mud balls at the museum. Instead, he drew pictures of Mr. Cavanaugh and then made marks across his ex-boss's face with a felt-tipped marker.

If you have had such revenge fantasies, you may worry that your thoughts are evil, or that you are a bad person. Not so. No one can read your mind, and thoughts that you don't act upon do not damage another person. The problem comes when you let the negative thoughts go on too long.

Sadness and disappointment came next. Brandon hadn't shed a tear for ten years, but when he woke up the next morning, he felt like crying.

Embarrassment, humiliation, and shame piled on top of his anger and sadness like layers of gummy frosting. He had told everyone he knew to come visit him at the cart. What was he supposed to tell them now? Brandon began to blame himself and to think of himself as a failure.

Rejection is a loss of expectations about how things were supposed to turn out. Grief is the process that comes after a loss. People who allow themselves to feel the various stages of grief eventually come to acceptance of the loss or the rejection.

How long we grieve is an individual matter. There is no right amount of time for it. Letting go of anger and other feelings about the rejection may happen gradually. Maybe you'll figure out a reason for what happened, but maybe you won't. However, you may wake up some morning and say to yourself, "All right already. I've had enough. Time to get on with my life." At this time, you have reached the stage of acceptance.

Feelings: Acknowledge, Express, Accept

Being aware of your feelings and giving them a name is an important first step in dealing with them. Go ahead and admit it. Say aloud: "I'm angry" or "I'm disappointed" or "I feel embarrassed." Remember to speak only about yourself and how you feel; you do not know how someone else feels. Speak the truth about your own feelings for the purpose of honest communication, not to hurt someone or to manipulate him or her.

If you've ever heard a person say, "I don't get angry," you know someone who is in denial or is lying. Anger scares some people because they consider it too violent. But anger expressed and handled constructively is neither violent nor destructive. People who try to deny their anger discover it often explodes later—when they are least expecting an explosion. Suddenly kicking the dog (or anyone else) is one example. It's cruel and will only make you feel worse about yourself later.

Besides naming and expressing your emotions, what are you supposed to do? Here are some techniques for dealing with the two most common emotions that follow rejection, anger and sadness.

Handling Anger: Be Careful—It May Be Hot or It May Be Cold!

Most of us think of anger as hot—red, sweaty faces; blowing off steam; a volcano erupting; a fire-breathing dragon. Anger can also be cold—giving people the silent treatment, refusing to speak, giving them the cold shoulder. But the ways of handling hot and cold anger are similar.

21

~ Stop and count slowly to ten. Never act in anger.

~ Get physical—in a healthy way. Leave the scene and run around the block, punch a pillow, shred newspapers, rearrange the furniture in your bedroom.

~ For hot anger, go to the bathroom, close the door, run cold water over a washcloth, and slap it on your forehead. Do this over again until you cool off. For cold anger, a warm washcloth on the forehead may help.

~ Go to your room and meditate. Sit on a chair with your feet on the floor. Take a deep breath in and let it out as you count to five. Repeat again as you concentrate on your breath. Keep your head clear of any other thoughts. Do not plan your revenge. (We'll talk more about meditation later.)

~ Write a letter or an e-mail to the person who rejected you. (You don't have to send it.)

~ Express your angry feelings to a good friend. If you can't find anyone to listen to you, talk to a lampshade or an empty chair.

Expressed anger is usually like the flaring of a match. But unexpressed anger can start a huge fire, or it can go inward and become chronic resentment festering long after the situation that caused the anger is over.

Max tells his counselor how it felt growing up in a family in which none of the members expressed anger. "No wonder my mother got migraine headaches. Whenever she got mad, she clammed up and refused to speak, sometimes for days. We tiptoed around waiting to see when she would let it all out. I remember the time she threw a four-pound box of powdered milk at the kitchen window. I'm not saying this is all her fault, but no wonder three out of the five kids in the family ended up battling addictions with tobacco and alcohol. We never learned how to express our anger."

No Dumping!

You've seen signs on empty lots that say "No dumping." But no dumping is also an important rule in the expression of feelings. Dumping can mean one or more of several things: Dumping can mean withholding feelings and tossing them much later at someone, blaming others and not taking personal responsibility for your actions, or using words like daggers or bullets to wound the other person.

No Best Way

So what is the best way to deal with anger? Here are some suggestions.

- Find the cause of your anger. For example, if you're ticked off because someone turned you down for a date, it's not fair to bite your mom's hand when she offers you a second helping of peas.

- Figure out what you can and cannot change. If you can't change the circumstances related to your rejection, you can at least learn to live with those circumstances. If you can change your circumstances, get to work on making those changes. For example, if you were rejected at cheerleading tryouts because you couldn't do cartwheels, you could learn how to do them and be ready for tryouts next year.

☞ You can confront the other person in a calm and peaceful way. First, state what you're angry about. Second, tell the person how you feel. Third, say what you would like to have happen. Propose a solution to the problem. Sometimes, you can do all three in one statement. Fourth, be prepared for the consequences.

Every summer the Cox family visited the grand-parents on a lake in northern Minnesota. And every day of the vacation since Lindsay was five and her brother was six, Grandpa had taken her brother fishing and left her behind. For years, Lindsay fumed over this injustice. She felt rejected.

The summer she turned thirteen, Lindsay decided to confront her grandfather. "It makes me sad," she said, "when Josh goes off fishing with you, and I have to stay here. I'd like to go, too."

"Why not?" said her grandfather. "Of course you can come. It never occurred to me that you would want to."

Sadness

It's All Right to Cry

Sadness is another natural reaction to rejection. Crying acts as a release and a comfort. Sometimes, in addition to tears, a short screaming fit may help. Make sure no one else is in the house (or warn those who are). Yell and stamp your feet. Have an old-fashioned temper tantrum. Pretend you're two years old again. Enjoy.

Are you an extrovert, someone who gets positive energy from others? Or are you an introvert, someone who prefers your own company? If being around other people perks you up, seek out a group or another person to hang out with. Doing something with people may be all it takes to pull you out of a rejection-induced slump.

If you're an introvert, it's okay to spend some time by yourself, nursing your wounds. Alone time becomes a problem only when you get too lonely and feel depressed about it. Be careful not to get into the "poor me" mode.

Erica felt that everyone seemed to be rejecting her—her parents, her brother, her friends, her teachers. She had spent some time alone just feeling her sadness, but that made her feel worse. Instead, Erica decided to pull herself out of the victim mode. She began making a list of the people who had treated her with kindness.

Be Kind to Yourself

➥ Choose a special treat just for you. It could be a good book, a CD, a fruit smoothie, a rose, or any other healthy thing you can think of.

➥ Do something nice for your body. Get some exercise. Take a shower or a bubble bath. Rub lotion on your skin. Get a massage.

➥ Write in a journal. Say nice things about yourself.

➥ Use your imagination. Using it in this way is sometimes called imagery. So you can't go to Hawaii. But you can imagine a sandy beach, lapping water or crashing waves, and the sun on your skin.

Depression: Sadness That Goes Too Far and Lasts Too Long

A rejection can make you sad, but if your sadness lasts too long and seriously disrupts your life, you may have clinical depression. Below are some of the symptoms of depression.

- Feeling sad, empty, or anxious most of the time

- Feeling hopeless, worthless, or guilty much of the time

- Sleeping too much or not enough

- Eating too much and gaining weight—or eating too little and losing weight

- Feeling restless and/or crabby

- Having various physical problems, such as headaches, digestive problems, or chronic pain

- Not being able to concentrate or make decisions

- Feeling tired and having low energy

- Thinking a lot about death and/or suicide

According to the American Medical Association, if you have four or five of these symptoms, including the first and the last, and you have had these symptoms for more than two weeks, you should see a mental health counselor. Even if you have only one or two of the symptoms, you might

26

benefit from a couple of sessions with a counselor. Some levels of depression require professional help.

Many people avoid getting help because they feel ashamed. They believe they should be able to solve their problems by themselves. But it's not shameful to get help. Almost anyone can benefit from an objective point of view. If you don't know where to go for help, call your local mental health association. Or you can consult a minister, priest, or rabbi trained in counseling techniques.

"I wanted to be an actress," Nikki says. "Instead of starting college right after high school, I went to an acting academy in California. There I am, all fired up to learn, and the first teacher I meet is Cora Flannigan. Even today, when I think of her I see her flaming red hair and the 'b' word comes to mind.

"Cora loved to intimidate and humiliate me. In her acting class, she used me as a pawn, spewing out her anger. She regularly embarrassed me in front of my classmates. Everything I did seemed to displease her.

"In a one-on-one conference, she asked me if I had ever had a CAT scan. I was shocked and said, 'No, why?' She said she thought I needed to have my brain tested. I swear to God, every word of this is true.

"I despised the woman but projected all of my hatred inward. When the year ended, I went home with my tail between my legs (so to speak). The experience sent me into a downward spiral. I felt like a total reject. My parents insisted that I see a counselor, a very understanding social worker they found out about. After a few sessions, I felt better and ready to apply to college. Now, about six years later, I'm a social worker myself."

27

As Nikki points out, the emotional pain that follows rejection can have a positive side. The symptoms of depression alert you to the fact that you need help. If you never acknowledge the pain, you may never get help. Another plus is being able to identify with (and maybe help) others who are having the same emotions you have had.

When dealing with depression, the best thing is to do something. Taking positive action of any kind may be enough to give your sad feelings a lift. For example, pick up the phone and talk to a friend or invite someone to go out to lunch.

Say No to Suicide

Often, people describe their feelings after a rejection as being as severe as physical pain. But a pain medication, such as aspirin, does not relieve them. Some people feel overcome by the urge to do something about the pain; they may view suicide as their only way out. But that is the wrong choice.

Many of those who commit suicide do so on impulse. "Relationship Cited in Case of Teen Who Shot Himself," says a newspaper headline. The story says a sixteen-year-old sophomore took a large-caliber handgun to the high school parking lot where he shot himself in the abdomen. Friends told school officials he had been disappointed over a failed relationship. However, interviews done with people who had reversed their suicidal thoughts revealed that most were very grateful they had not acted on impulse.

Those who consider suicide after a rejection believe they have no other options. But they do have options, and so do you. If you feel actively suicidal (in other words, find yourself making plans for suicide), do any of the following immediately:

➥ Call 911.

➥ Call or go to a local hospital.

➥ Find a crisis intervention service or suicide hotline. You can get the number from Information (411) or from the yellow pages of your telephone book.

➥ Get in touch with a community mental health center, which you can find in the government listings of the telephone book. (If you have previously worked with a mental health counselor, this is the time to get reengaged with that person.)

➥ Try not to be alone. Find someone who will stay with you. Ask him or her to listen to you.

➥ Get rid of guns. If there are guns in your home, ask your parents to lock them up.

➥ Don't drive. If you're feeling suicidal, the impulse to drive recklessly and/or too fast may be stronger than you think.

Increase your use of meditation and relaxation techniques. It's difficult to feel depressed when you're meditating. Useful affirmations (positive statements about yourself) will sound something like these (say these statements over and over until you begin to believe them):

☞ "I want to live."

☞ " I choose life."

☞ "There is still much for me to live for."

Think about it: Would you want to give the person who rejected you so much control over you that you choose to end your life? Remember that you are not a reject just because someone has rejected you.

Love Those Feelings

Feelings (or emotions) are important parts of ourselves. Feelings make us alive; feelings make us human. From our emotions we learn a lot about ourselves. Loving our feelings, both positive and negative, is an important part of loving ourselves.

When in Doubt, Check It Out

When we assume too much, we get ourselves in trouble. We assume a person made a sarcastic remark to hurt us. We assume two people got the giggles because of us. We assume "those people" raised their eyebrows about us. And we assume that everyone sees the world in exactly the same way we do. They don't.

Samantha grew up in Ohio with her cousin Tyler. Both were only children, and their mothers were sisters. Samantha felt she could tell almost anything to Tyler, and he would understand.

At the beginning of Tyler's junior year in high school, his dad got transferred to New Jersey. Samantha felt terrible but imagined they would keep in touch by e-mail. At first, when Tyler didn't answer her "letters," Samantha assumed he was busy adjusting to his new surroundings. She tried to be patient and upped the interest level for her cousin by asking him lots of questions.

On Thanksgiving weekend, he sent her a brief reply without answering the questions or asking her any. Finally, Samantha decided to check it out. "Are you mad?" she asked. "Did I say something wrong?"

About a week later, Tyler answered. "Why would I be mad?" he wrote. "Of course you didn't say anything wrong. I thought you knew that I am a terrible correspondent." After this, Samantha felt sad but relieved to know that her cousin wasn't rejecting her.

Asking questions may feel like a giant step that requires great courage. You may want to wait for the right moment, but the right moment never comes.

Jeremy had never had a relationship with a girl. In fact, in his nineteen years, he'd had only a few dates. He met Dawn in a speech class at his community college and asked her if she wanted to go out for coffee. She did, and they had a great time. Dawn was friendly, peppy, cute, and had a great sense of humor. After a few dates, Jeremy began to think of Dawn as his girlfriend.

One Saturday he invited her to a family barbecue. "I'd love to come," she said, "but I have other plans." When Jeremy went to the grocery store to pick up some chips, he saw Dawn with a guy. Jeremy felt so hurt, so rejected, he immediately stopped calling her.

After about a week, Dawn called Jeremy. "What happened?" she asked. "Did I do something wrong?" Jeremy explained that he'd seen her with a guy at the grocery store.

Dawn laughed. "Did he have a shaved head? That was my cousin from Indiana. He left today."

Jeremy realized that he could have saved himself a week of misery if he had only checked it out.

If you do wait, is it too late to talk about the situation that made you feel rejected? No, it's never too late. Just say, "Remember when . . . ?" Or you may say, "I've been thinking about . . ."

You may worry that checking things out will make the situation worse. Hasn't your mother always told you not to hurt another person's feelings?

Maybe you worry that the other person won't tell you the truth for fear of hurting your feelings. However, nothing ventured, nothing gained. You'll probably discover that bringing up the subject in a calm, polite way will make the situation better, not worse.

Kate, a high school junior, expected to get the part of Adelaide in the high school's fall musical, Guys and Dolls. Two days after the audition, she consulted the call-back list. She couldn't believe what she saw—or didn't see. No Kate on the list. Nowhere. Eventually, a girl who couldn't even sing got "her" part.

Later that day, choking back tears as she thought about her rejection, Kate went home. Her mother suggested she check things out with the drama teacher. Even though Kate liked Ms. Miller (or had liked her up until now), she felt silly assuming she should have had the part. She thought long and hard about what to say—or if she should say anything.

The next day after class, Kate stood up and said to herself, "Well, here goes nothing." She marched up to Ms. Miller's desk. "Um . . . I was wondering . . . is there something I could have done better?"

Ms. Miller smiled as if she could read Kate's mind. "Of course, there's always something a person can do better, but you did very well. Keep in mind, though, that this is a public school, and everyone deserves a chance to perform."

33

Kate nodded. She understood.

"Believe me," Ms. Miller went on, "keep showing up for auditions. Your time will come."

It did. Kate got the lead in the spring musical.

It took guts to confront a teacher about the rejection situation, but Kate was glad she had done it. She realized that if she hadn't checked it out with Ms. Miller, her resentment would have continued to simmer. Maybe she wouldn't even have auditioned for the spring musical.

Sometimes, it's the wording of a statement that you need to check out.

Jane worked hard at her summer lifeguard job. She always came on time—even when she had to open at 6:30 AM. She never read or talked to friends during her shift; she kept her eyes on the kids and on the adult lap swimmers. She kept the pool clean and picked up the litter around it. She called all of the regulars by their first names.

One day, in front of a group of people, Jane's supervisor remarked, "Jane is one of my most compulsive guards."

Compulsive? The word had a harsh, negative sound. One of Jane's friends had obsessive-compulsive disorder and took medication for it. The remark made Jane feel hurt and rejected.

The next day she decided to check it out with her boss. "I was wondering why you said that about me," said Jane. "You said I was compulsive. It didn't sound too good."

34

Her supervisor laughed. "Would you feel better if I said you're the best guard I've ever had? I appreciate all the extras you do, like picking up litter around the pool. I apologize. I meant my remark as a compliment."

Remember, there are effective ways and ineffective ways to check things out. One not-so-good way, but one we often use, is to put people in their place with "you" messages, which come across to the other person as blaming. No one likes being blamed. The other person gets his or her defenses up and responds with another "you" message directed at you! Here's an example of a "you" message.

Sam's mother: "You never listen when I'm talking and you always interrupt."
Sam to his mother: "You never say anything I'm interested in hearing."

Here's the same conversation translated into "I" messages.

Sam's mother: "When people interrupt me, I feel discounted, unimportant. I would feel better if the people I'm addressing would look me in the eye and let me finish talking."
Sam: "Okay. I can try to be a better listener. But it's important for me to feel as if I have good ideas, too."

"I" messages take a bit of practice, but you'll find they're worth the trouble. People can't read your mind, after all. Letting them know what you want and need is the essence of good communication.

Alex (to his older brother): "When we couldn't play tennis after we'd agreed to, I felt pushed aside."

Brad: "I was afraid of that. But my girlfriend was available to go camping only on Saturday."

Alex: "I still feel sort of second-best. I can't compete with your girlfriend."

Brad: "I apologize. I'll make it up to you. I promise not to cancel the next time."

After this exchange with his older brother, Alex still felt disappointed, but he also felt heard and understood.

When you communicate with "I" messages, it's important that both people agree to really listen. Active listening is a process with a built-in mechanism for checking it out. One major part of active listening is to ask the other person to repeat back to you what he or she heard you say, including what the other person thought you meant.

In the above example, Alex asked Brad, "How do you think I felt when you canceled out on our tennis date?"

Brad thought for a minute and then said, "I guess you felt sort of unimportant."

"You got it," said Alex. "Thanks for listening."

Another step in active listening is to try to put yourself in the place of the other person. Alex knew that Brad's girlfriend, Tiffany, was a year older than Brad, and that his brother felt somewhat insecure about the relationship.

Sooner Rather Than Later

Tara belonged to a church group that met approximately once a month. She'd written "hike" in her calendar for the upcoming weekend, but no one had called to invite her.

On Thursday, she saw her friend Brittany at the mall. "Aren't we supposed to go on a hike this weekend?" Tara asked.

"Didn't Derek call you?" Brittany said. "He called me, but I can't go."

Tara tried not to show her sense of rejection. Maybe Derek had called all of the other people (the more important ones), discovered they couldn't go, and canceled the hike. All weekend Tara felt sad.

On Monday, she saw Derek at school. Why hadn't she called him right after she talked to Brittany, she asked herself. Because she felt scared and hurt at the rejection. At the time it seemed easier to nurse her wounded feelings than to do something about them. But now she wanted to find out. Better late than never.

"I felt left out," she said to Derek, "when you didn't call me about the hike."

Derek frowned. "I did call you. On Tuesday, I think it was. I left a message on your voice mail."

"I didn't get it," said Tara. "I bet you left it at the wrong place."

"Bummer," said Derek sincerely. "I wondered why you didn't call me back. We had the hike with three people, but it would have been more fun with you."

While Tara wasn't happy about missing the hike, she was glad she'd checked it out. Checking things out helps you avoid one of the most common responses to rejection, taking it personally, the subject of the next chapter.

Don't Take It Personally

When we take it personally, rejection hurts. The trick is to find ways to keep from taking it personally.

Rita has a summer job as a waitress. She tries to be prompt and accurate with her service and cheerful in her attitude. And yet, some people are rude and crabby. In the first week, Rita almost quits. She feels rejected by many of her customers. But she tells herself that hunger makes folks irritable. She refuses to take their attitudes personally.

What's Wrong with Me?

On Monday morning Seth lost his house key, on Monday afternoon he burned his fingers taking a cup from the microwave, and on Monday night he stubbed his bare toe on the bed frame. "What's wrong with me?" Seth yelled.

We do tend to take rejection personally. But was the rejection really our fault or does the problem lie with the "rejecter"? In many cases, the rejecter is envious of the other person or believes he or she can build up his or her own self-esteem by hurting someone else. Other types of rejection may come from thoughtlessness or prejudice.

One of our goals is to see what we can do to change the situation without taking on a load of self-blame. We need to take a serious look at the event without letting self-blame take a bite out of us.

Don't Reject Yourself

Have you ever bitten into a wormy apple? Only a part of the apple is affected, but you toss away the whole thing. When you feel rejected, the same sort of thing happens. Stop and consider the circumstances. Never throw yourself away. When you become more accepting of yourself, you will be less likely to take rejection personally. (We will talk more about self-acceptance in chapter six.) You can choose what you want to do. Do you want to end your relationship with the rejecting person? Do you want to ignore the incident? Do you want to be a doormat and risk further rejection? Do you want to talk to the person about it? Do you want to make another effort at friendship?

Tiffany still hasn't completely figured out what happened on the senior trip to Washington, DC. She takes comfort in telling herself that what went wrong may not have been entirely her fault.

Although she and her best friend, Olivia, had different roommates, they interacted in the large group activities. One day, Tiffany was organizing seven people, including Olivia, who wanted to explore the city on their own.

39

At one point, Olivia cut down Tiffany by saying, "Girl, you talk so much no one else can get a word in!"

For a moment, Tiffany felt as if Olivia had slapped her. Speechless, she plopped into a chair in the corner. No one else seemed to notice, which made Tiffany feel even more rejected. A few minutes later, Tiffany heard Olivia saying, "Okay, kids. Time to get off your butts. When can everyone be ready? Where should we go?"

If she hadn't felt so furious, Tiffany would have laughed. Here was Olivia doing the very thing for which she had criticized Tiffany. As she sulked her way through that day and into the next, her friend Chaz tried to make her feel better. "Don't take it personally," he said. "It's her problem, not yours."

After a rejection, we may overreact by denying everything. This doesn't allow for the acknowledgment, acceptance, and expression of feelings. Unacknowledged and unexpressed feelings may cause trouble. On the other hand, we may find ourselves taking all of the blame for a rejection. We tell ourselves such things as "I'm no good," "I'm stupid," or "I totally screwed up." This type of negative self-talk not only fails to help, it actually makes matters worse.

Negative Self-Talk

We all talk to ourselves—in our heads. If you don't believe it, spend a day "listening" to yourself. If you have time, write your negative messages in your journal where you can take a look at them later. Following are some common rejections that people give to themselves on a daily basis. Do any of these messages sound familiar?

Mind Reading

Can you read someone else's mind? If so, you have a gift that few others have. But if you just think you can read minds, your self-talk may be disastrous to your mental health.

Example: He didn't call me at 8 PM. He must be blowing me off.
Actuality: Maybe he's in the library doing his homework. Maybe he's out with his parents. Maybe he's stuck in traffic. He has a life. He doesn't have to call me every night.

Overgeneralizing

This is the error of making broad generalizations based on only one shred of evidence.

Example: I didn't get a part in the play. Therefore, I'm a lousy actress and should stop auditioning.
Actuality: I didn't get a part in the play, but I had a big part in the last one. Someone else deserves a chance.

Catastrophizing and Awfulizing

Telling yourself that everything happening is a major disaster is catastrophizing; sometimes we call it awfulizing.

Example: He broke up with me; therefore, I'm a reject and will never have a relationship with anyone ever again.

Actuality: It's probably good we broke up. We weren't right for each other, but I was hesitant to say anything.

Shoulds

Shoulds are rigid rules that say how everyone, including you, should act. When you talk to yourself in "shoulds," you are setting yourself up for rejection and/or failure.

Example: I should never get angry.
Actuality: I probably need to get angry once in a while. Anger is a normal human emotion.

Personalization

When you think that the world revolves around you, then everything that happens reflects on you and your self-image.

Example: He probably didn't call me after homecoming because he thought I was boring or ugly or both.
Actuality: His parents made him invite someone. They said he had to get a date for homecoming if he wanted them to pay for driver's ed. He had a good time at the game and dance, but he's not ready for a long-term relationship with anyone.

Author and counselor Penelope Russianoff calls negative self-talk an emotional bad habit. Like anything a person repeats over and over, constant negative responses become habitual. Just as a person can become addicted to cigarettes or alcohol, a person can become addicted to being rejected. Good feelings about ourselves get easily blown away by the negative.

Remember the story of Jessica, eighteen, who had the relationship with the twenty-three-year-old guy? Before she looked in the mirror and told herself she was better off without Tom, she had taken it personally. She had made the following negative statements to herself: Maybe I came on too strong; maybe I didn't give him enough space; maybe I wasn't sophisticated enough; maybe I'm too fat; maybe I wasn't friendly enough to his friends. In all of these self-questioning statements, Jessica blamed herself for being rejected. Then she realized the truth. Although she wasn't perfect (who is?), Tom's own issues (the use of alcohol and drugs) caused the breakup.

Sometimes, the reason for what seems like a rejection becomes apparent long after the fact.

Everyone in Sadie's English class liked Ms. MacIntosh. Almost everyone called her Ms. Mac or Mac. She was young and peppy and had a way of making even Shakespeare seem interesting. Sadie paid attention in class, turned in her assignments on time, and did careful rewrites. She worked hard for Ms. Mac. As a result, she felt she had a special relationship with her teacher, who often gave her an affirming look or a pat on the shoulder.

Sometime in the spring, though, Ms. Mac started to joke around with her less often. Several times she sort of snapped back an answer when Sadie asked her a simple question about an assignment.

Sadie began to wonder what she had done wrong. She rarely said anything bad about Ms. Mac to anyone, but maybe she'd complained about a grade to someone, and Mac had overheard her. Sadie felt rejected by one of her favorite teachers and took it personally.

Two weeks before the end of school, a substitute for Ms. Mac told the class that their teacher's mother had died after a long illness.

"No wonder she didn't seem to like me anymore," said Sadie. "She had more serious things on her mind. But I kept thinking it was something I did."

If not taking rejection personally was simple, you could stop reading now. But the job of depersonalizing is not a simple one. You may have to take many more steps before you become immune to the stings of rejection.

Here is a short list of tips to help you keep on track.

- Imagine yourself wrapped up and protected in bubble wrap. Stay there until you can get enough emotional distance to deal with the situation.

- Remind yourself that you are not the center of the universe. Other people have needs and wants, too. Try to put yourself in that person's shoes. Sometimes, a simple talk will clear up misunderstandings.

- Ask yourself how much of the problem is yours and how much belongs to the other person.

- Say to yourself aloud or in your head, "Don't take it personally." Say this sentence over and over, as many times as it takes to persuade yourself that whatever happened wasn't all your fault.

Forgive Yourself and Others

To forgive is to "pardon an offense or an offender" or to "cease to feel resentment against" (*Merriam Webster's Collegiate Dictionary*). But forgiveness is more than the dictionary definition.

- Forgiveness is the key to healing and a way to avoid becoming filled with bitterness.

- Forgiveness is a way to get over rejection and to quit being a victim.

- Forgiveness is letting go of the past.

- Forgiveness is a gift to someone you believe has done you wrong.

- Forgiveness is a gift to yourself.

- Forgiveness is a way of getting rid of the anger that otherwise stays bottled up inside you.

- Forgiveness is nonjudgmental.

- Forgiveness is a deep breath followed by a feeling of relief.

Forgiveness may be a difficult concept to wrap your mind around. It may feel impossible until you recognize the benefits to you. What forgiveness is not:

- Forgiveness does not mean you have to announce it to the world or to those you have forgiven. Even without your announcement, they will probably notice the difference in your attitude.

- Forgiveness does not mean letting the person get away without confrontation or consequences. A person who commits a crime against you may have to serve jail time. But you can still forgive that person.

- Forgiveness is not denying your pain or any of your other feelings, including anger. However, people who have complained of chronic headaches, stomachaches, and other aches after a rejection often notice that the pain disappears when they forgive.

- Forgiveness does not require you to heal a relationship.

Max's mother (mentioned in chapter 2) suffered from bad migraine headaches. She's the one who once got so angry that she threw a box of powdered milk and broke the kitchen window. Much later, she stumbled upon information about forgiveness. "I think a more forgiving attitude would have helped my migraines," she said. "The replacement window cost me a bundle, and the whole process used up a lot of valuable time. Plus, my behavior embarrassed me. Forgiveness would have been a better option."

46

Brandi enjoyed spending time with Kim, a girl new to the school. She invited Kim over for dinner and included her in group activities with friends; she even remembered Kim's birthday. But Kim never thanked Brandi for the special things she did. After Kim didn't even mention the birthday card Brandi sent her, Brandi said, "Forget her. I've tried hard enough."

Weeks passed. When Brandi had a party, she planned to leave Kim off the list. But one Sunday in church, Brandi's minister preached a sermon about forgiveness. Without expecting anything in return, Brandi invited Kim to the party. Two days later, Kim called. "Thank you for hanging in there with me," she said. "A lot of people would have given up. I was on an asthma medication that made me feel tired all the time. I'm on a new medication now, and I feel like a different person. Would you like to go to a movie?"

Why Hold On to Anger?

Many people do not realize that forgiveness is an option. They've seen their parents and grandparents nurse their anger for years. They have never considered how much better forgiveness would make them feel.

Harrison's mother's feud with her only brother had gone on so long that she didn't even know what started it. She hadn't spoken to her brother for about ten years. When Harrison graduated from high school, he wanted his uncle to come to the ceremony. When his uncle showed up, he and Harrison's mom hugged each other and cried. "I forgive you," said Harrison's mom. "I don't

47

even remember what you did, and I don't care. I feel so much better now."

Some people would rather be right than be happy. Some people believe that in order to forgive, they have to assign blame to someone. These people live in a black-and-white world. In reality, the world comes in many colors, as well as in shades of gray.

They enjoy the role of martyr or victim. When people act like victims, other people tend to feel sorry for them and make a fuss over them—for a time. But after a while, people begin to see through the martyr role to the insecurity underneath.

They are so used to their own feelings of anger and negativity, they feel "undressed" without them. They believe that if they hold on to their misery, they won't have to take the risk of getting hurt again. They may be scared to share their intimate thoughts and feelings because they think that if people get to know the real them, they'll be rejected again. They believe that anger makes them more powerful. They think of it as a jet engine that makes them go.

What Good Is Blame?

Some people treat their pets better than they treat themselves. They get angry at themselves when their performance does not measure up to some imaginary standard. Do you expect perfection in others? No? Then why expect it of yourself? Has it ever occurred to you to forgive yourself?

Young children see themselves as the center of the universe. When something goes wrong with the universe, it's their fault—or so they think. When parents get divorced, their children wonder what they did wrong. Children who are neglected and abused believe they themselves are flawed. Why else would such terrible things happen to them?

Some parents expect perfection. We've all heard the story of the high school student who brings home three As and one B on her report card, only to have her parents say, "Why did you get the B?" Also, some parents actively teach children that self-love is wrong and end up teaching low self-esteem. For many, negative habits feel comfortable because they are familiar.

Forgive

In order to get over it and stop the self-blame, you need to develop a new mind-set. Judy Tatelbaum, author of *You Don't Have to Suffer*, suggests stopping yourself every time you make a self-blaming statement. If you hear yourself saying, "I'm so stupid," stop and ask if you can forgive yourself for whatever you did and also for that remark. If you can, say aloud, "I forgive myself now and at all times in the future."

Ted says, "My younger sister Kelly was really popular in high school. She had tons of friends. I had one or two at most. I was so jealous of her I could taste it. Because of my envy, I made her life miserable. I need to apologize to her and to myself."

Kelly says, "I had no idea Ted felt jealous of me. I always looked up to him because he was older and so smart. I thought he rejected me because I wasn't his intellectual equal. I believed that Mom and Dad were disappointed in me because I couldn't do math to save my life. Of course, I couldn't reject my parents. Instead, I told myself I was stupid and cut my brother out of my life. I owe him an apology."

With understanding, Ted and Kelly were able to forgive each other.

Empathy: Walk a Mile in Someone Else's Shoes

Empathy means seeing a situation from the other person's point of view. Seeing rejection from the "rejecter's" point of view may enable you to forgive that person.

One of the main reasons people reject others has to do with their own limitations, which include childhood wounds, lack of knowledge, frustration, and fear. When you forgive someone who has rejected you, you see beyond your pain into the pain of the other person.

Letting Go of the Past

Most of us rerun past hurts and rejections through our brains like old movies. Sometimes "playing it again" helps us make sense of what happened. But more often, hanging on to painful events keeps us from moving forward with our lives.

Megan talks about her ten-year high school reunion. "My strongest memories of high school, especially of the social scene, are negative. Even

50

though I tried hard to fit in, high school was the pits. For example, one day at lunch, my friend and I (I did have one friend) sat down at the most popular clique's table. Immediately, the clique girls got up and left. I felt so embarrassed—like a reject.

"If the people at the reunion measure success in terms of money, education, profession, and marriage, then I'm still a flop. But I don't consider myself a failure. I have a job with benefits, a place to live, and some new friends. I'm not doing so badly.

"I forgive those girls, and I've forgiven myself. I did the best I could at the time, and so did they. They were all insecure. That's why they stuck together and wouldn't let anyone else in.

"Now I can look back at that time without getting knots in my stomach. But I'm still not going to the reunion. I have a date, and we're going bowling."

Forgiveness Exercises

Forgiveness sounds simple—just do it—but it takes work. Judy Tatelbaum suggests an exercise you can use when trying to forgive yourself or someone else.

Get a big piece of paper and list (with spaces in between) all of the people with whom you have a relationship. Put your own name at the top of the list.

As you move down the paper, ask yourself if there is anything in each relationship you cannot forgive. For example, what about your relationship with yourself? Can you forgive yourself for rejecting your grandmother in the months before she died? You didn't mean to neglect her, but you did. What a way to treat a person who had given you so much! Include all of your feelings about what happened. If your grandmother were still alive (and that's the problem; she's not) you could go to her and ask for her forgiveness. In her absence, however, you can substitute an empty chair—or you can ask someone to play the role of your grandmother as you beg her forgiveness. You can imagine her saying, "Of course, I forgive you." At the same time, you can say to yourself, "I forgive you, Self, for your thoughtlessness. I have learned something and will try to treat others with more kindness in the future."

You can repeat this for the other people in your life. If your friends are available, talk to them. If not, talk to the empty chair or to a picture of the person. Or you can write the person a letter, which you do not have to send. Remember Tiffany and Olivia, who took the senior trip to Washington? Tiffany never actually said these words to Olivia, but she did write them in her journal. "I apologize for feeling resentful about your remarks to me on the trip. I forgive you."

The Role of Stress

Stress in our lives occurs whenever we have to adapt to change. Distress is negative or bad stress. Eustress is the name for positive or good stress. What one person considers bad stress another may perceive as good.

Take moving, for example. Your dad is transferred from San Diego to Chicago in the middle of your junior year of high school. He sees this transfer as a great career move: stress, maybe, but good stress. You see it as a disaster. You tell your dad you won't go. Leaving your friends would cause you too much distress. Your distress causes your dad distress in turn.

Most people believe it's the way you look at your stress that determines the effects. There's some evidence that negative responses to stress can actually predispose a person to physical illness. Finding ways to recognize and deal with your stress can make you a strong person in the same way that a broken bone gets stronger after it heals.

How to Deal with Stress

Personality characteristics such as optimism and hopefulness help people cope with stress. People also find a strong spiritual faith and the support of others helpful. In addition, there are other steps to take. We will discuss more of these in the chapters that follow. For now, file this tidbit away in a corner of your brain: Not being able to forgive can cause stress.

Forgiveness is a state of mind. To live in a state of forgiveness is to practice forgiving every day of your life. Say these words over and over: I forgive others. I forgive myself.

Accept Yourself

What Is Self-Esteem?

Self-esteem, also called a positive self-image, is liking yourself, feeling good about yourself—just as you are. Self-esteem is a deep belief that you are okay no matter what anyone else says to you or about you. A well-known family therapist, Virginia Satir, talks about "high pot" and "low pot." If your self-esteem is high, your pot is full, and you can give to others. If your self-esteem is low, your pot may be nearly empty, and you will not have much to give to anyone.

Where Do We Get Self-Esteem?

Self-esteem begins in childhood. If your parents seemed pleased with you and gave you unconditional love, chances are you grew up liking yourself. However, sometimes even well-meaning parents give negative messages to their children. Why? That's the way their parents raised them; they don't know any better. They are not pleased with themselves. Rather than trying to improve their own self-esteem, they do a number on you. They think that by giving you negative messages about yourself, they are changing you for the better. Actually, the opposite is true; they are probably lowering your self-esteem.

54

Here are some examples of negative messages parents and other well-meaning adults give to children. "You're growing like a weed." "No, you can't have any more ice cream; you're getting too fat." "Stand up straight; you're getting round-shouldered." "What a terrible haircut. It looks like a butcher did it."

Negative message: Peggy's mother never trusted her to return her own permission slips to school. She was sure Peggy would lose them.

Negative message: When Jim was eleven years old, his mother was still picking out his school clothes for him. She was afraid he would wear the wrong things and embarrass her.

What if Peggy did lose her permission slip? That would be her problem and she would learn from the consequences. What if Jim did wear the wrong clothes and the kids teased him? That would be his problem and he would learn from the experience. When parents protect their children too much, they cause them to have low self-esteem, which makes them more vulnerable to rejection later in life.

Positive message: When she was ten years old, Joanne's parents let her take a job walking the neighbors' dog.

Positive message: Andrea's parents included her in the dinner-making schedule. They each made dinner twice a week. On Sundays, they went out to dinner together.

Parents with high self-esteem allow children to take responsibility. They let them make mistakes and learn from them. High self-esteem helps people face rejection.

Position in the Family

Another possible influence on self-esteem is your position in the family. An oldest child might develop high self-esteem because of his experience in caring for the younger children. On the other hand, if his parents constantly criticize him for the way he treats the younger children, his self-esteem will sink. A youngest child may feel well-loved. But if people in the family consider her the baby, incapable of taking responsibility, her self-esteem may suffer. If your family gives negative messages, you can become aware of these messages and resolve not to accept them.

Reject Me!

Henry sits at the bus stop wearing his "Reject Me" T-shirt. He hasn't taken a shower for three days, he never combs his hair, and his shoulders droop as if he's carrying a fifty-pound backpack. Henry stares at the ground. He has low self-esteem, and he looks "rejectable."

Although a casual observer can't always guess your level of self-esteem, some people seem to ask for rejection. If you feel bad about yourself, chances are it will show. Other people will pick up on your low opinion of yourself and treat you accordingly.

Carrie loved her friend's yellow skirt with the blue and white flowers. "Felicia," Carrie said one day,

56

"how come you never wear your yellow skirt with the flowers anymore?"

"Oh," said Felicia, "I gave it away. It was too bright, and people always stared at me when I wore it."

Some people make the mistake of thinking they are the center of the universe, but Felicia had the opposite problem. Because of her low self-esteem, she considered herself unworthy of anyone's attention.

Putting yourself down verbally is another bad habit that indicates low self-esteem. How would you react to the following common rejection experiences?

Broken Relationship

Negative response, indicating low self-esteem: "No wonder he broke up with me. Who could love me? I'm not pretty and, besides that, I have a lot of bad habits."

Positive response, indicating high self-esteem: "Dating Al was okay, but we spent so much time together I lost a lot of my girlfriends. Now I'm going to call some of them and reestablish our connections."

Work-Related Rejection

Negative response, indicating low self-esteem: "I was excited when I got the job as a busboy. But two weeks later, they let me go. I guess I'm just incompetent."

Positive response, indicating high self-esteem: "Two weeks after I got the job, they said they had hired too many people. Business had slowed down. I believe what they told me, that they'll give me a good reference. I know I won't have trouble getting another job."

Accepting Yourself and Others

When you have high self-esteem, you accept yourself, warts and all. And when you like yourself, other people will like you, too. When you are accepting of other people, they tend to accept you.

"Oh, no," Jonelle screams. "Don't take any more pictures of me. I'm all nose, eyebrows, and hair. I never want to see a picture of myself again." When anyone tries to take a photo of her, Jonelle covers her face with her hands and ruins the picture. If she didn't call attention to her nose, eyebrows, and hair, no one would notice them. But Jonelle, obsessed with what she considers her negative features, cannot love herself.

Because of Sasha's experiences with rejection as a child, she tends to expect rejection and to minimize acceptance. When Sasha received an award for organizing a blood drive, she threw the certificate away. "It was nothing," she said. "It didn't really matter."

Author Ken Wilber says that one of the most common complaints of people seeking therapy is that they feel rejected. They say no one likes them, or that people are critical of them. However, many of the same people deny that they themselves are critical and rejecting of others. Wilber suggests that those who feel rejected take

58

a close look at themselves and work at being more accepting of others.

Self-Esteem: How to Get It

If you don't already have high self-esteem, how do you get it? Even if you don't believe in your own value, pretend that you do. If you act as if you believe in yourself, you may actually start believing in yourself.

➭ Try smiling. When you go out in the morning, smile at people. Many will look away, but others will smile back and/or start talking to you. The positive responses you get from others will help you feel better about yourself.

➭ Dwell on the good. Most people tend to accentuate the negative. If three good things happen to you on any given day and one negative thing happens, the negative will probably weigh more heavily in your mind than the positive. Concentrate on the good things instead.

➭ In your journal or notebook, write down the times each day when you have accepted yourself (as is) and when you have felt accepted by others. How did you feel about being accepted? Did you maximize or minimize your good feelings?

➭ Help others. Helping other people helps you. Remember, though, that while you're helping others, you don't want to neglect yourself. You'll be effective only if you feel good about yourself.

➭ Be yourself. Do what you want to do, not what someone else expects you to do.

59

➭ When you have a bad day in which your self-esteem is low, remind yourself that everyone has such days. Everyone makes mistakes. Look at your list of acceptances and successes. Focus on the positive.

Learn to Accept Compliments

"I'm polite," says Carrie. "If someone gives me a present, I always write them a thank-you note." But when someone gives Carrie a compliment, she usually minimizes it.

Carrie's friend: "I like your new dress."

Carrie: "Oh, it was a hand-me-down from my cousin. It's kind of ugly."

Carrie needs to learn to smile and say "Thank you" when someone gives her a compliment. Learning to accept compliments graciously is an important part of self-acceptance.

Be Your Own Best Friend

To do this, you need to get to know yourself. A good way to start is by keeping a journal or a notebook about your thoughts and feelings as a self-confident, capable person. Make different sections in your notebook for the following:

Needs

Ask yourself what you need to be content? A dish of ice cream every night? A best friend? A part-time job?

Accomplishments

What have you accomplished in the last year? In your life? In this section you might want to record your skills, such as sports, art, computers. Or you can record the things you've done to help others, such as volunteer projects through church, or helping your parents by doing family errands or baby-sitting for younger siblings.

Goals

What do you hope to accomplish in the future? In this section include short-term goals, such as cleaning your room or your locker at school, inviting a friend over, or offering to cook dinner for the family. Long-term goals could include going to college, buying a car, saving some money, understanding the meaning of life, or learning how to cope with rejection.

As you think of new needs, accomplishments, and goals, add them to your notebook. This activity will help keep you focused on your strengths.

Be kind to yourself. Remember that you cannot change certain situations. You cannot change other people. You can change only yourself and your reactions to situations.

Never Compare Yourself to Others

One symptom of low self-esteem is constant comparing. Give yourself a test. Notice how many times a day you compare yourself (usually negatively) to one of your friends instead of accepting yourself for the unique individual you are. People with low self-esteem envy other people. There is no end to the things they envy: Erik is more athletic; Suzie has a better figure; Carl has lots of money; Cassie has a handsome boyfriend; Glen is so smart.

Avery is always comparing herself to someone else, and she never measures up. Yesterday, she compared herself to her outspoken friend, Maddie. Maddie has an opinion on everything and never hesitates to express it. In fact, she writes editorials for the school newspaper. "I could never write an editorial," says Avery. "Most of the time I don't know what I believe. I usually see two sides to every question."

Today, Avery compared herself to her friend Evie. Evie likes to tell Avery how she should live her life. "You shouldn't go out with Ken," says Evie. "He's a real loser. He's always putting you down."

In the first instance (Avery's relationship with Maddie), Avery needs to recognize that her ability to see both sides of an issue is a gift. Not everyone needs to write editorials. In the second instance (Evie), Avery needs to consider that no one can put her down except herself. And only she can decide if she wants to continue her relationship with Ken. Or, for that matter, her relationships with Maddie and Evie.

Say to yourself: "I am me. I am unique. I am lovable. I am kind. I've had successes. I keep trying. I love me."

Even if you practice all of the above suggestions, higher self-esteem may take a while to achieve. Do what you believe is honest and right for you. Remember that even if you lose some of life's battles, you still want to have your self-respect.

You Can Overcome (the Fear of Rejection)

What do Beethoven, Barbra Streisand, Winston Churchill, Madonna, Walt Disney, and Thomas Edison have in common? You guessed it. Rejection.

A teacher told the great composer Ludwig von Beethoven he would never make it as a composer. Entertainer Barbra Streisand's stepfather told her she was ugly. British Prime Minister Winston Churchill had to repeat sixth grade. Singer and movie star Madonna grew up feeling like an outsider in her own home. Moviemaker Walt Disney once lost a job at a newspaper for not having enough ideas. Thomas A. Edison, inventor, was told he was too dumb to learn.

Keep Trying

The famous people above and many others overcame rejection. When no one else believed in them, they believed in themselves. When they failed, they tried again.

Art Mortell, the author of *The Courage to Fail*, insists that the fear of failure is more upsetting than failure itself. He adds that you should expect to get rejected at least 30 percent of the time. Otherwise, you aren't trying hard enough.

Have you ever noticed that the more often you make a trip, the less time each trip seems to take? We've already learned that a broken bone gets stronger at the place of the break. It's the same with rejection. Welcome rejection, swallow your fears, and go for it. A sign in front of a church says, "We Don't Fail; We Just Quit Trying."

Beth says she's getting to be an expert at accepting and learning from rejection. This spring she plans to audition for a musical theater program at a prestigious university. One of the drama department's stages has a ceiling that moves for improved acoustics. In spite of probable rejection, Beth wants the experience of singing on that particular stage—under that ceiling and in front of those lights.

Consider the Alternatives

What happens to people who do not keep trying, who allow the fear of rejection to rule their lives? They let the past rule the present and believe that they can't do anything. People don't often choose to become victims. Instead, they let the victim role pick them because they don't take any positive action.

For example, someone invites you to go to a party. Three days before the event, the person calls and breaks the date. Of course you are angry. But you can choose to nurse your anger and stay home and sulk. Or you can find someone else to go to the party with you. Or you can go alone and meet people there.

Fear of rejection can affect all areas of a person's life— relationships, school, and work. Sitting around waiting for the fear to go away won't work. For example, you've been asking girls out for a couple of years. Is there any magic number of girls you have to talk to before the lump in your throat disappears and your heart stops pounding? Probably not. The only positive action is to get a move on and do the things you're afraid of doing, even though you might experience rejection again.

Tips to Get You Going Again

Go ahead; say it. "I'm scared." It's important to admit and confront your feelings. Also, try writing your feelings down. See the words on paper. Art Mortell says we must express our feelings. If we don't, we allow rejection to become our enemy. We get depressed and have no idea why.

Second, evaluate your fear. If you try again, is there anything you can do to minimize your chances of failure? If it's an audition, can you get better prepared? If it's a job interview, can you ask yourself some expected questions?

Third, allow yourself a "worry period" each day. Don't let the fear of rejection color every moment or seep into every cell of your body. Instead, pick a ten- or fifteen-minute period each day in which you give yourself over to feeling your fear. If you find yourself worrying at any other time of day, switch off those thoughts until your worry period.

Fourth, instead of concentrating on the worst things that could happen, allow yourself to visualize success. What pictures appear in your head? Maybe it's scoring the winning goal in a soccer game. Maybe it's being elected treasurer of the student council. Maybe it's getting an A in geometry. Whatever it is, think positively. Write each day's successes in your journal.

Fifth, practice gratitude. If you pray, add thankfulness to your prayers. "I'm grateful for my health, for my parents, for my friends, for my dog, for my cat, for my house." You get the idea.

Finally, make yourself take at least one non-life-threatening risk every day. Ask yourself this question: "If I try again, what is the worst thing that could happen?" If your answer is, "I could get rejected again," ask yourself the next question: "If I fail, will I die?" No? Then why not try again?

You probably think that the best possible thing that could happen to you is success. But sometimes the best thing that can happen is rejection and the lessons you learn.

Saying Yes (or When Life Hands You Lemons . . .)

In chapter 2, we talked about allowing ourselves to feel our emotions. In chapter 4, we said, "Don't take it personally." Do these two pieces of advice contradict each other? Not really. The key to survival is not the pain, but how we react to the pain.

Four senior girls got stuck without dates to homecoming. All felt the pain of rejection. Two of the girls sat alone in their houses that night. They made themselves, and everyone around them, miserable. The other two girls organized themselves into a decorating committee. They took on a job no one else had time to do. They had fun. At an all-school assembly the next week, these girls got a service award and recognition for a job well done.

Saying yes to life after a rejection does not mean you don't feel the pain. You do feel it, but you allow yourself to look at the good rather than concentrating on the bad.

> *Sandy auditioned for plays at her school and never got anything but a tiny part. She tried to believe the words of her drama teacher: "There are no small parts, only small actors."*
>
> *"Baloney," said Sandy, and she cried into her pillow at night.*
>
> *But Sandy didn't give up. She accepted her small parts, contributed extra hours to set design, and enjoyed hanging out with the drama club kids. Before her junior year, Sandy's teacher recognized her creativity in design.*
>
> *Sandy's drama teacher saw to it that Sandy went to college on a scholarship. Five years after graduation from college, she's a well-known set designer in New York.*

Keep Your Eye on the Prize

Ask yourself an important question: "How badly do I want the prize?" If you want it badly enough, you have to keep trying. We could call this rule "I'll show them!"

> *Naomi graduated from high school at age sixteen and went to a local college. Although she had no great interest in joining a sorority, some of her friends were going through rush and urged her to join in. Soon Naomi found herself caught up in the social scene. When the time came to declare choices,*

Naomi put down two choices even though she wanted only sorority number one. As things turned out, she only got an invitation to join sorority number two.

The rejection by her first choice hurt so much, Naomi felt as if someone had given her a punch in the stomach. She got on the phone, called her mom, and sobbed. However, an hour after that conversation, Naomi promised herself she would make sorority number one sorry they hadn't chosen her. Naomi distinguished herself at college. She made dean's list every quarter, was elected president of her senior class, and lettered four years in swimming and volleyball.

At age fifteen, Aaron was a serious wrestler, but at the state level, he lost his match and was ready to give up. "I tried with every ounce of energy I had," Aaron said. "I just couldn't do it. Now I'm imagining everyone is pointing at me and calling me a loser. I feel like a loser; I feel like I'm nothing."

Aaron's coach told him that anyone who has ever achieved greatness has tried and failed, but the winners are those who keep trying. They identify their weaknesses and work at correcting them. They don't give up.

Just remember, though, that while there's nothing terrible about working hard to show them, you really want to achieve something to please yourself, rather than to try to please someone else.

Grow with the Flow: Making Positive Changes

You have decided to welcome rejection—or at least not to dread it. At the same time, you're trying to make other positive changes in your life. Do you think you can change? You can!

Assert Yourself

"I don't want to be aggressive," says Monica. "I can't stand aggressive people."

Assertive does not mean aggressive. Aggression implies pushing one's way into someone else's territory. An assertive person is not pushy but quietly self-assured. Assertive people are self-confident but not obnoxious. They are polite, but they speak with authority and don't need excess words.

Sometimes, these different styles start at a young age. Let's listen to an exchange in a day-care home. Andy picks up Billy's dump truck and starts moving it across the rug.

Unassertive Billy: Goes to the corner, cries, and stares daggers at his friend.

Aggressive Billy: "Gimme that!" (Grabs truck.)

Assertive Billy: "I need to have my truck back, please. Here, you can play with this fire engine."

In the final exchange of words, assertive Billy is clearly in charge. He asks for what he wants, and he gets it.

Michaela admires her assertive friend Fran. If Michaela invites Fran to come over and Fran can't make it (or doesn't want to), she says simply, "I have plans."

When Michaela gets an invitation she can't or doesn't want to accept, she goes into long explanations that sound phony. "Well, I'd like to come over, but we have to pick my grandmother up at the airport, and then I have to wash my hair, and then it will be too wet . . ."

Assertive people don't need to make long explanations or talk loudly. They expect that people will listen to them.

Sixteen-year-old Liz is trying to become more assertive. She is beginning to recognize how she comes across to others. The sound of her own voice on the answering machine makes her cringe. "I sound like a baby," she says. "Well, maybe not like a baby— more like a six-year-old."

Your posture is important, too. If you stand with your shoulders slumped, your hand over your mouth when you speak, and your eyes on your shoes, no one is going to want to listen to you. Instead, when you talk, stand up straight, shoulders back. Make eye contact with the other person, and speak clearly and with authority.

Sometimes, being assertive means not accepting rejection.

Hannah is a groovy, gorgeous eleventh-grade girl. Karen is quiet, serious, and shy. The girls grew up together, their parents were friends, and Karen's mother was their Girl Scout leader. But Hannah rarely acknowledges Karen's existence.

Recently, an old friend, Charity, who had moved away in fifth grade, moved back to town, and Hannah organized a gathering. Karen heard about it from one of Hannah's friends, not from Hannah herself. Karen felt left out; she thought of asking Hannah if she could come.

After a few hours of feeling sorry for herself, Karen decided to act assertively. She would organize her own party, include people who had been left out of the other party, and invite Charity.

Taking action made Karen feel powerful and much more assertive than usual. Her feelings of rejection melted away. Busy with her own party plans, she forgot about Hannah.

Look Your Best

You don't have to spend a lot of money to look nice. Taking care of your teeth, your hair, and your skin does not have to be expensive.

Paula buys all of her clothes at thrift shops or next-to-new stores. When people ask Paula where she got that nice outfit, she tells certain people the truth. Her answer to others might be "At a special store," "I can't remember," or "My mom bought it."

The way you look on the outside is not a measure of your inner worth. But if you take the trouble to look nice, you are telling yourself and the rest of the world that you are worth the effort.

It's Not the Decision, but the Way You Live with It

You will have times in your life (everyone does) when things don't work out as planned. You had hoped to get that summer internship, but your best friend got it; you had hoped to get elected class secretary, but you didn't make it; you had hoped to get into X University, but no dice. You had no control over these rejections; they happened and that's that.

But you do have control over what you do next—how you handle the rejection. Philip C. McGraw, author of *Life Strategies: Doing What Works, Doing What Matters,* says that you are the person who makes your life work. Sometimes, you will make a decision that clicks, that looks more and more right as time goes on. But some decisions will not look right, and you will have to work at making them right.

When Naomi (from chapter 7) didn't get into the sorority of her choice, she cried. Sorority number two made relatively few demands on her time. "This is good," said Naomi to herself, "because I want to keep my eye on the goal, the reason I'm in college." Naomi enjoyed having fun, but she also wanted to go to medical school. She was able to put academics first and social activities second.

72

Many years later, working as the pediatrician she had always wanted to be, Naomi considered her rejection from sorority number one. "The rejection wasn't my decision," she said, "but what to do next was. I tried to make things work. I don't know if I'll ever get over the pain of that rejection, but in many ways, it was the best thing that ever happened to me."

Be Healthy

A healthy lifestyle works like a vitamin pill for the soul. You don't have to do everything at once. All you have to do is take a few baby steps. The following are suggestions to make a healthier you.

Don't Worry: Be Happy!

Experts say that optimists, people who look on the bright side of life and believe good things will happen to them along the way, live longer than pessimists, people who look on the dark side. After a rejection, you may feel like a pessimist; you may feel down. But staying down, being a pessimist, will not do you any good. Which of the following two young men do you think will have an easier time in life?

Jake: "Girls don't like me. They think I'm a geek. Why should I try? I'm a loser."

Walt: "Maria said she couldn't go to the movie with me. Maybe I'll ask Susan. I'm sure I can find someone."

Optimists usually have the following characteristics:

↪ They keep smiling even when things get rough.

↪ They look on the bright side of any situation and don't dwell on the negative.

↪ They see themselves as being able to control most aspects of their lives.

↪ They expect their lives to be generally happy. If something bad happens, they see it as an isolated incident.

↪ They set realistic, attainable goals.

↪ They keep trying.

↪ If they do have to give up in certain instances, they tend to accept the rejection as for the best.

↪ They realize it could be worse.

Laugh a Little; Laugh a Lot
Scientists have shown that laughter and play have physical and emotional benefits. As you look back over your rejections, can you find anything funny about any of them?

Jerry still believes that the soda pop incident contributed to his rejection by Amanda. He had invited her to a romantic picnic by the lake. He brought smoked salmon and crackers. On the way home, he opened a diet soda, which exploded all over him and his date. The next day, Amanda called and broke up with him. Although the whole thing seemed totally unfunny at the time, Jerry can laugh at it now.

Here are some suggestions to keep you having fun.

- Surround yourself with people who make you laugh and feel good about yourself.

- Call up someone you like and make a date with that person. Plan something both of you will enjoy.

- Fill an empty shoebox with things that make you laugh or smile—jokes, cartoons, e-mail messages.

- Put funny things on your bulletin board, your bedroom walls, the bathroom mirror, or the refrigerator.

- Have a fun-sharing time with your family as often as you can.

- Try to find something funny in all of the irritating things that happen to you each day.

Alisha is the receptionist in the law office in which Tad has a summer job. The day after vandals broke into the office, smashing windows and overturning desk drawers, Alisha put on her curly blond wig and large rubber nose while she made calls to the police and insurance company.

People may think they are funny when they tease you. They may be trying to elevate their own low self-esteem by putting you down. On the other hand, people tend to joke around with folks they like. Usually, the best way to deal with teasing is to laugh at yourself and ignore the remarks. If the teasing is hurtful or mean, tell people that their nasty remarks don't hurt you but reflect badly on them.

Work Out

Exercise is good for your body, but even better, it makes you feel good. Physical activity energizes endorphins, the body's natural painkillers. If rejection has dampened your spirits, exercise will lift your mood. "But I'm depressed," says Jane. "I don't feel like working out. I'm just so hurt. I'll have to wait until I'm feeling better."

If you wait until you feel like exercising, you may wait forever. Start now. Start small with fifteen minutes a day, then work up to thirty minutes. Build an exercise routine into your day as a must do. Are you a morning person? If so, set your alarm fifteen minutes earlier than usual. Go for a walk. Don't let yourself eat breakfast until you get back. If you're not a morning person, do your walk before dinner.

Choosing the kind of exercise is less important than whether or not you do it. Some people do exactly the same thing every day. They like the routine of a thirty-minute walk or swim. Others like cross-training and vary their routines with something new every day, such as shooting baskets or hitting tennis balls.

If you're having trouble getting started, try to find an exercise partner. If you can't find anyone, consider joining a class. Community school catalogs may list classes in the following sports and physical activities: racquetball, volleyball, basketball, gymnastics, soccer, flying trapeze, dancing (ballet, ballroom, Argentine tango, salsa, mambo, swing, modern, jazz, hip hop/funk), aerobics, cardio-kickboxing, swimming, and tennis.

Eat Well

You are what you eat. This old expression contains some truth. After a rejection, you may feel tempted to eat foods that taste great going down but that make you feel heavy and sluggish—hot fudge sundaes, greasy fries, salty chips, and fast foods of all kinds.

But comfort foods do not have to be bad-for-you foods. Try snacks of air-popped popcorn, low-fat fruit smoothies, or raw veggies with low-fat dressing. Pick as many of your foods as possible from healthy food groups, such as fruits, vegetables, grains, and legumes. (Legumes include beans, peas, lentils, chickpeas, refried beans, tofu, tempeh, and soy milk.)

Get Enough Rest

Crawling under the covers after a rejection may work for a few hours, but it's not good as a regular habit. To get over a rejection, you need to engage with life, not hide from it. Experts say you need seven or eight hours of sleep (not much more, not much less) every night.

Ever since his girlfriend broke up with him, Will has gotten in the habit of taking a long nap after school. Sometimes he gets up in time for dinner; sometimes he doesn't. Usually he wakes up by 8 PM. He then stays up until 3 AM, watching television. He drags himself out of bed the next morning, but he's often late for school. After school, he's tired. Then he needs his nap.

Will's doctor told him to break this habit by cutting out the afternoon nap. No naps at all until bedtime at 10 PM. Will's sleep pattern has had a negative effect on him because he's not available for interactions with friends after school. He doesn't participate in extracurricular activities or exercise, both of which would make him feel better about himself and his rejection.

Here are some tips for a good night's sleep.

- ➥ Exercise every day for at least thirty minutes.

- ➥ Do not eat late-night, heavy meals or snacks.

- ➥ Don't drink caffeinated beverages after 3 PM. (Better yet, don't drink them at all.)

- ➥ Don't drink alcohol, which may put you to sleep, then wake you up in the middle of the night.

- ➥ Don't smoke. Nicotine is a stimulant.

- ➥ Go to sleep imagining a pleasant scene with you in it. Do not play the rejection over and over in your head.

- ➥ Keep your bedroom at a comfortable temperature, not too hot and not too cold.

- ➥ If you have trouble getting to sleep, play soft music or listen to relaxation tapes.

- ➥ Set your alarm and get up when it rings.

Get Busy

Most people agree that if you want something done, ask a busy person. Busy people are "doers." They don't sit around moping about their rejections for a long period of time. They don't dwell on their past but look forward to their futures. Keeping busy propels them to accept new challenges.

What about you? Is there something you've always wanted to do that you haven't tried? Want some ideas? A community school catalog listed the following classes: "Creating Greeting Cards from Your Photos," "Dog Obedience," "Beginning Sculpture in Clay," "The Art of Collage," "101 Ways to Paint a Picture," "Tae Kwon Do," "Ikebana—Japanese Flower Arranging," "Beginning Scrapbooking," and "Stop Smoking and Never Start Again."

Maybe you'll decide it's time to help someone else. Volunteering is sure to give you a lift. Do you like being outdoors? How about trail building and maintenance with the Nature Conservancy or the Sierra Club? Do you like working with old folks? How about reading to people in a nursing home or writing letters for them? Do you like working with your hands? Maybe Habitat for Humanity can use your help. Try the art museum, public library, churches, hospitals, schools, soup kitchens, and homeless shelters.

Relax

After a rejection, you may feel angry, resentful, and uptight. "Just relax," someone says. But relaxation may be easier said than done in your frantic life. How do you begin?

Relaxation techniques work, but they take time and practice to learn. A good way to get started is to sign up for a course on stress relief, relaxation, or meditation. Try a local community school, YMCA or YWCA, Jewish community center, or Buddhist center.

You can also go to your public library or bookstore and get some books and tapes. You might want to put on your headset and follow the directions of an audio tape, such as "Meditation for Beginners" by Jack Kornfield, "How to Relax" by Patricia Carrington, or "The 10-Minute Stress

Manager" by Emmett E. Miller, M.D. There are several book sugggestions in the For Further Reading section at the end of this book.

Meditate

"I don't have time to do anything," says Zach. "I'm too busy. I'm going about fifty miles an hour all the time."

We all have busy lives, and it is important to keep active. But it's also important to slow down and catch your breath.

Meditation is the practice of getting rid of thoughts and worries that clutter your mind. There are many ways to meditate, though all take practice. You should have no trouble finding a course or book on the subject.

One of the most basic ways to keep yourself focused is to concentrate on your breath. First, breathe slowly in, counting to seven as you inhale. Then exhale as you count to seven again. When you breathe, only your abdomen should move noticeably, not your chest. When you get into the rhythm, say the words "inhale" and "exhale" in your head in time to your breathing.

Be Mindful

Being mindful is another type of meditation. Mindfulness means paying attention. You can be mindful of your breathing as in the previous exercise. Or you can be mindful of what you are doing throughout the day. You may find mindfulness difficult in this era of multitasking, such as talking on your cell phone while driving the car. Suddenly you arrive at your destination (if you don't crash into someone on the way) and wonder how you got there.

Mindfulness may include waking up at dawn and feeling the ache of rejection. At the same time, you may be able to appreciate the pink and orange of a beautiful sunrise.

Yoga

Any of the many different types of yoga will help you learn to breathe deeply and gently stretch your muscles. Your body will become stronger, and your posture will improve. Best of all, yoga will make you feel relaxed and, at the same time, energized.

Tai Chi

This Chinese martial art is an exercise system for relaxation of body and mind, as well as a self-defense discipline. *Tai* means "pole" or "center point." The five major styles of tai chi cultivate *chi*, or the body's vital force. Because tai chi is among the most popular of movement arts in the Western world, you should have no trouble finding a class or practice group.

Imagery

Use your imagination to picture a situation the way you think it should be. Imagining a desirable outcome may become part of making that positive outcome real. This technique is known as visualization.

Before Kate confronted her teacher, as described in chapter 3, she pictured herself walking to the front of the room and making eye contact with Ms. Miller. She rehearsed her speech. Picturing this scene ahead of time, called visualization, helped Kate go through with checking things out.

In stressful situations, imagery and visualization can help you relax. What kind of daydreams do you have? Do you picture yourself on the busiest street corner in the city, breathing exhaust fumes? Or do you see yourself on a white-sand beach with waves lapping at your toes? Your daydreams can give you a mini-vacation from stress.

Progressive Muscle Relaxation

Progressive muscle relaxation is a simple exercise in which you tense and relax various body muscles. Total relaxation is your ultimate goal.

Lie down or sit in a comfortable, quiet place. Start with your head. Wrinkle your forehead. Hold that frown for five seconds. Relax. Squint your eyes. Hold them closed for five seconds. Relax. Press your tongue against the roof of your mouth for five seconds. Relax. Squeeze up your nose like a rabbit. Hold. Relax. Clench your teeth. Hold. Relax. Purse your lips as if you're kissing someone you don't like. Count to five. Relax. Pull your head back so far that you stretch the front of your neck. Hold and relax.

Keep working down your body, tensing and relaxing various muscle groups. Pull your shoulders up against your ears. Hold for a few seconds, then relax. Press your chin against your chest. Hold and relax.

Tense and relax your abdominal muscles. Do the same for your rear end. Arch your back. Hold for a few seconds; relax. Bend your feet toward your waist. Hold. Relax. Now try to make your toes touch the ground. Hold. Relax.

When you get proficient at progressive muscle relaxation, you can do it almost anywhere.

Massage: You Knead It

For thousands of years, people have used massage for tension reduction and to increase feelings of general well-being. In the past quarter of a century, this ancient therapy has become even more popular. Nowadays, more than a hundred methods are classified as massage therapy.

A professional massage may cost more money than you have. If that's the case, you can find a friend who is willing to knead (as in making bread) your tense back, neck, and shoulder muscles in return for a massage from you. Or you can try your local school. At one community school, a certified massage therapist teaches "Back, Neck, and Shoulder Massage" as a one-evening course.

Avoid Unhealthy Distractions

"He tried to drown his troubles in drink." We've all heard that expression. If only our painful feelings would die so easily. But they won't. As we already know, the way to deal with painful feelings is to feel them and then let go of them.

People who haven't learned to appreciate their feelings, especially painful ones, often turn to substances such as alcohol and drugs to try to get relief. They hope to avoid the pain. "Numbing" may seem to work for a while. But alcohol and drugs only make matters worse. It's like the medication a dentist gives you to deaden a tooth. After the dentist fixes your tooth and the numbing effect of the medication wears off, the pain is still there.

And, of course, alcohol and street drugs can lead to addiction. An addiction of any sort, from drinking too much to playing too many computer games, adds problems on top of problems. When the temporary relief wears off, the pain of rejection remains.

If you do get in trouble with drinking, using drugs, or other addictions, you may need the help of a counselor or a twelve-step program, such as Alcoholics Anonymous or Narcotics Anonymous.

Break Unhealthy Relationships

Relationship experts warn that if you have experienced rejection in early childhood, you may continue to look for rejection in your current relationships. Rejection does not feel good, but at least it's familiar. However, as your self-esteem improves, you will find yourself asking, "Who needs this?"

While you're making positive changes in your life, make a decision to break the pattern of unhealthy relationships as well. Instead of hooking up with people who will let you down, find those who will lift you up. Instead of the familiar but unhealthy rejecting relationships, find healthy relationships with those who appreciate you unconditionally.

Get Spiritual

Being spiritual doesn't necessarily mean subscribing to specific religious teachings. Spirituality may be as simple as believing in a higher power. Medical experts have shown that people with religious faith and practice tend to have better health than those without faith. Spirituality can help you cope with rejection by helping you see the big picture. There are many different kinds of spiritual practices and prayers. Prayer can help with healing, forgiveness, and hope. Remember to pray in thanksgiving for what you have, especially for your valuable relationships.

The Value of a Fighting Spirit

Jared is a junior in college, majoring in film. After he sweated for weeks over a screenplay, his professor commented, "I don't like it; write another one." Jared went back to work and created a second script. He waited anxiously for his professor's reaction. "It's garbage. The first one wasn't very good, but it was better."

Jared considered dropping the course or even changing his major. But his fighting spirit took over. "I'll show him," he said to himself. He cranked out play after play and turned them in. At their final conference, the professor and Jared sat across from each other. Jared waited for the ax to fall.

It didn't. "You've come a long way," said the professor. "I'm expecting great things from you. Keep up the good work." Jared got an A in the course.

Get Support

The Power of Confiding

When rejection strikes, you need someone to talk to. Telling your story to a trusted friend helps. Everyone needs at least one good friend. But after a rejection, your feelings about what happened ache to get out and be heard. You may need more than one good listener. Otherwise, you risk burning out your main support.

The low-energy period after a rejection isn't the best time to start new friendships. After you've recovered from a rejection—and before the next one—is a good time to reach out and cultivate new friendships. Make sure you

85

learn people's names, take the risk and invite someone to have lunch, or suggest a walk or a bike ride.

Don't forget your family. Get to know your parents, siblings, aunts, uncles, and cousins on a more intimate level than "Please pass the butter." Reach out to others in the family. Invite them to talk to you when they have problems.

As mentioned previously, writing is also a good way to get it all out. Don't worry about your grammar, punctuation, or spelling—just get it down. What if you're not a writer? Try a tape recorder. Talking to a tape recorder can provide useful feedback, especially when you listen to yourself months or years later.

Find a Support Group

If a rejection makes you feel so crummy that nothing else seems to help, you may find a support group useful. One of the advantages of such a group is hearing the stories of others with problems similar to yours—or even worse. The support of a group decreases feelings of loneliness and isolation. You'll meet new and understanding friends and learn what has worked for others. Another advantage of a support group is cost—some are free or inexpensive.

You may be lucky enough to find a support group that deals specifically with postrejection issues. The classified section of a neighborhood newspaper might say, for instance, "Affordable counseling offers support groups for those dealing with the loss of a relationship. Groups meet every other Tuesday and are led by a therapist. A $15 fee for each meeting and a four-week commitment are required."

If rejection or unhappiness have caused serious or long-term problems such as alcohol or drug abuse, try a twelve-step group such as Alcoholics Anonymous or Alanon. Recovery, Inc., is a support group for those with depression or anxiety. For more information, consult your telephone book or see the resource list at the back of this book.

Time to Get Counseling?

Do you think your reactions to rejection have gone on too long or have caused you too much distress? Ask yourself the following questions. If you answer yes to most, you may want to consider getting extra help.

- Do I feel like crying much of the time?

- Do I feel lonely even when I'm with people?

- Do I sleep a lot (or have trouble sleeping)?

- Do I eat too much or not enough?

- Do I feel irritable and blow up for no reason?

- Do I have trouble making decisions?

- Do I feel as if I have no friends?

- Do I have trouble getting necessary things done?

- Do friends or family members say they're worried about me?

- Have I used harmful substances, such as cigarettes, alcohol, or drugs, to numb out or alter my mood?

- Have I ever thought of suicide?

87

Counseling (psychological therapy) may seem like a last resort, but it doesn't have to be. However, for any kind of therapy to work, you have to want it to work, you have to believe it can work, and you have to do some of the work. Even those who take medication because of anxiety and depression have to put forth some effort in therapy.

Types of Therapy

Peer Counseling

The therapy that works for you may be as uncomplicated as peer counseling, also called cocounseling. Find a friend and agree about how often you want to get together, at what time, and for how long. (Most people meet for an hour once a week.) Divide the available time in half. During your half, you get to talk about anything on your mind, except for anger at your partner. Your cocounselor will listen and give supportive feedback. When your talking time is up, switch places with your partner. Now your partner will do most of the talking as you become the counselor, the listener, and the advice-giver.

Sometimes, seeing how you come across to others is enough to snap you out of the rejection/victim stance.

Ashley started her senior year in high school at the same time her best friend, Taylor, started her freshman year in college. Ashley sent daily e-mails to Taylor, expressing her feelings.

After about a month of communication, Taylor wrote to Ashley. "Thanks for the mail, but every other sentence you write has the word 'depressed' or 'depressing' in it. I'm getting depressed just listening to you!"

88

Ashley felt the sting of rejection and reacted with anger. She didn't write to Taylor for two weeks.

As time passed, however, Ashley began to see Taylor's point. She had been too negative and downbeat. She decided to write again to her friend detailing funny things that had happened at school. She asked more questions about Taylor's college experience. The correspondence resumed.

Cognitive-Behavioral Therapy

One type of problem-solving therapy is called cognitive-behavioral therapy. Cognitive therapy has to do with changing how you think about a situation. Behavioral therapy may help you change self-defeating actions. Put the two therapies together and you have a mechanism for behavior change. The underlying principle behind these types of therapy is that even something as hurtful as rejection does not cause as much distress as the way you think and behave after the rejection.

Thought-stopping is a useful technique anyone can practice after a rejection. Instead of thinking "I'm so unlovable" or "I must be a loser," think such thoughts as "I will learn from this experience," or "This is not the end of the world."

If you can do positive thinking and acting on your own, go for it. Otherwise, you can get the help of a therapist to give you a push in the right direction.

Choosing a Therapist

Trust is the main ingredient in any therapeutic relationship. You will need to believe that your therapist can help you change your outlook on life for the better. Therapists have different ways of working. Before you get started with a therapist, be sure to ask the person about his or her style.

Your health insurance may limit your choice of a counselor and the length of coverage. If you do have a choice, don't be afraid to try out several counselors before choosing one. Some therapists do not charge for the initial session; others do.

Here are some questions to ask yourself before you choose a therapist.

➭ Is it important to have a therapist close to home?

➭ Do I want a same-gender therapist?

➭ How young (or how old) do I want my therapist to be?

Here are some questions you might want to ask the therapist or counselor.

➭ Do you like working with people my age?

➭ Do you think you can help me?

➭ How do you think you can help me?

➭ How many times will I have to come?

➭ How long is each session?

➭ How far in advance do I need to change my appointment or cancel it?

➭ What do you charge and what will be the arrangement for payment?

Types of Therapists

The most common types of counselors include psychiatrists, psychologists, and social workers. Also, ministers, priests, and rabbis are helpful.

Psychiatrists are medical doctors who have finished medical school plus several years of residency training. They are certified when they pass the examination of the American Board of Psychiatry and Neurology. Psychiatrists are the only mental health professionals who can prescribe medication and order medical tests. They will have the initials "M.D." after their names.

Psychologists are doctors of psychology with the initials Ph.D. or Psy.D. after their names. They do counseling and testing.

Licensed clinical social workers also act as counselors. They have master's degrees in social work plus extra supervised experience in doing therapy with clients. The initials M.S.W. stand for master of social work; L.C.S.W. stands for licensed clinical social worker; and L.I.S.W. stands for licensed independent social worker.

Getting the Idea

By now you're probably getting the idea that a rejection does not have to be the end of the world. In fact, a rejection may turn out to be the beginning of a new and better world for you.

Now It's Your Turn: How to Reject Someone (If You Have To)

So you thought getting rejected was tough. Just wait until you have to do the rejecting! If you haven't yet been a "rejecter," you will no doubt have this experience in the future.

Nothing Lasts Forever

Understanding that nothing lasts forever will not only help when you feel rejected but will make you feel better when you have to do the rejecting. Even your grandparents, married for sixty years, will have to deal with the end of their relationship when one of them dies. And people who have had one job for their entire lives will eventually retire.

Most of us need practice in letting go. Some people are so afraid of the fallout from rejection that they cling to relationships and jobs even when such clinging is unhealthy for themselves and others. Some unhealthy and unsuccessful coping mechanisms include the following.

Denying

People may deny that their negative feelings exist. Although it is hard to take the responsibility of being the rejecter, that role may actually be easier than the role of the rejected.

Delaying

Fear of separation keeps some people miserable in jobs they hate or in unhappy relationships. Because they fear being the rejecter, some people put off the inevitable. Young people who continue to live at home long after they are financially independent are one example of delay.

Incompletely Separating

Some people are unable to complete the separation. Take the relationship between Kurt and Natasha. Two weeks ago, Kurt told Natasha he thought they should break up. But he kept calling her and asking her to come over. Natasha knew why Kurt was calling, but she went because she hadn't yet found another relationship.

While it's nice to forgive those who have rejected you, or even to stay friends with them, this kind of incomplete separation can be unhealthy if it keeps both parties from moving on to more satisfying relationships.

Not Separating at All

We have all seen examples of grown-up children who have never left home. By this time, they're adults, and they are usually unhappy with the arrangement. They let it go on because they are afraid to separate or because their parents are afraid to "reject" them. Couples who stay together for the sake of the children are another example.

Fleeing

We may read a story that tells of a person who has mysteriously vanished. Years later, the vanished person shows up alive and well in another city. In many cases, the person who disappeared may have been trying to avoid rejecting someone else.

Although rejecting another person is rarely easy, you can reject in healthy ways.

Have Compassion

Remember the golden rule: Do unto others as you would have them do unto you. When you have to reject people, consider their emotions.

"I don't want to get rejected," says Sally, "but if it has to happen, I would like the person to say something nice before dropping the bombshell."

"If it's going to happen," says Gus, "I want it to happen sooner rather than later. Especially in a dating situation."

"I want honesty," says Roy. "I don't want the person to make up a whole lot of lies to spare my feelings. With honesty, maybe I can learn something."

Dan's parents didn't like his friend Evan. In fact, they told Dan that Evan was not permitted to come to their house. Furthermore, they would prefer that Dan not hang out with Evan at all.

When Dan thought back, he had to admit that Evan was the person who'd driven his parents' car out of the garage and around the block for a joyride when both of them were fourteen. But Dan didn't want to hurt Evan's feelings by rejecting him.

When the boys got arrested for shooting Evan's BB gun at 3 AM, Dan changed his mind. After his appearance in juvenile court, he delivered the rejection directly. "We're not good for each other," Dan said. "I think we should find other friends."

Face the Truth

Although there may be occasions that call for sugarcoating the truth, honesty is usually the best policy. Tell the truth in a way that shows respect for the other person's feelings. Usually, that person will appreciate your honesty and be able to handle it.

Keep Communication Open

Straightforward communication of emotions is closely related to facing the truth (above). Letting the other person know that you are sad, too, helps both of you. Hurting from the pain of rejection, the other person may not have thought of your pain. Your relationship in its present form may end, but you may still be able to stay friends. Sharing sad feelings along with anger, happiness, resentment, and appreciation facilitates the healing process.

In her book, *Making Friends with Yourself and Other Strangers*, Dianna Daniels Booher suggests other ways to end a friendship—when there is no other alternative.

➢ Sometimes, tapering off is the answer. Rather than an outright rejection, you can decrease the intensity

95

of the relationship by spending less and less time with your friend.

⮑ As you back out of the friendship, you can help your friend find other people who can help him or her or to whom he or she can relate. If the person has been dumping on you, maybe you can refer your friend to someone else, such as a counselor or a teacher.

⮑ Try to make the breakup as painless as possible by saying something nice and remembering the good times. For example, "I've enjoyed your friendship, but we seem to be going in different directions."

Plan Ahead

Many aspects of life work out better with advance planning. The unpleasant task of having to reject someone is no exception. You will need to do some planning on the macro (large) level, as well as on the micro (smaller) level to decide if you want to reject someone.

On the Macro Level

When you do your planning related to the big picture, ask yourself the following questions.

⮑ Will I be better off without this person in my life? This question sounds harsh, but remember that you can't take care of anyone else unless you first learn to take care of yourself.

⮑ If I reject this person, how am I going to deal with the consequences? Realize that you may feel just as bad for a while afterward as the person you've rejected. Can you put some plans in place to take care of yourself?

➥ If I reject this person (especially in a romantic relationship), am I prepared to stick with my decision and make a clean break? (If both parties decide to stay friends, that's okay as long as one person doesn't have unrealistic hopes of rekindling the flame.)

On the Micro Level

Planning on the micro level includes the details of your plan, such as when, where, and how you are going to drop the bombshell. If you believe you will have difficulty carrying through with your plan, try picturing a place for your meeting and setting a date. Write the date in the calendar. Planning for the "how" could include some role playing with a friend or a parent. Imagine what you will say and what the other person might say in response.

Is It Ever Okay to Tell a Lie?

"I think it's okay if you stretch the truth a bit to keep from hurting someone's feelings," says Mindy. "I mean if there's no other way to reject a person gently, a little white lie might be okay."

People who always tell the absolute truth can cause terrible hurt. For example, in breaking up with Tessa, Julian might tell the absolute truth: "Actually, Tessa, you're a lot of fun, but you're not that pretty." This type of honesty is just plain mean.

97

Sometimes, lying can get you into trouble.

Allison has had two dates with Ray. Ray invites her to go to a movie on Saturday. "You know what, Ray? I'm not interested in having an exclusive relationship with anyone right now." Two weeks later, someone tells Ray that Allison and another guy are going out.

Pam invites Kyle to the Sadie Hawkins dance. He says, "I'm sorry. I have to go visit my grandma out of town that weekend." Pam invites someone else. Kyle shows up at the dance with the cocaptain of the girls' soccer team.

If you're going to tell a little white lie to keep from hurting someone's feelings, be sure you don't get caught with your hand in the cookie jar.

A Part of Life

Rejection is a normal part of any life. Whether you are the rejected or the rejecter, you can handle it—if you are prepared.

98

Glossary

abandonment The act of completely forsaking someone or something.

addiction Compulsive, uncontrolled dependence on a substance or activity.

aggression An offensive action, assault, or attack.

antidote Something that counteracts unwanted effects.

assertive Confidently self-assured.

clique A small, exclusive group of people.

compulsive Repetitive behavior done in response to obsessive thoughts.

coping mechanism A way of facing and dealing with problems.

empathy The ability to identify with and understand the feelings of others.

endorphins The body's natural painkillers.

family therapist A counselor who focuses on improving the interactions among family members.

imagery The formation of positive mental concepts to promote health.

immune Resistant to infectious disease.

manipulate To influence or skillfully manage, often in an unfair manner.

migraine headache A recurring, throbbing vascular head pain.

obsessive Having persistent thoughts the mind has trouble getting rid of.

predispose A tendency or inclination to something.

racism A belief, policy, or system of government that espouses the idea that one's own race is superior to others.

rejection A refusal to accept or recognize.

tai chi A nonaggressive martial art from China that uses relaxation and yielding techniques.

vulnerable Capable of being hurt.

yoga A system of breathing techniques, stretching postures, muscle movements, and meditation.

Where to Go for Help

Alcohol and Substance Abuse

Alcoholics Anonymous (AA)
General Service Office
Grand Central Station, P.O. Box 459
New York, NY 10163
(212) 870-3400
Web site: http://www.aa.org

Narcotics Anonymous (NA)
World Service Office
P.O. Box 9999
Van Nuys, CA 91409
(818) 773-9999
Web site: http://www.narcoticsanonymous.com

National Clearinghouse for Alcohol and Drug
        Information (NCADI)
P.O. Box 2345
Rockville, MD 20847-2345
(800) 729-6686
(301) 468-2600
Web site: http://www.health.org

National Council on Alcoholism and Drug Dependence
    (NCADD)
20 Exchange Place, Suite 2902
New York, NY 10005
(212) 269-7797
Web site: http://www.ncadd.org

Substance Abuse and Mental Health Services Administration
    (SAMHSA)
An agency of the U.S. Department of Health and
    Human Services
5600 Fishers Lane
Rockville, MD 20857
(301) 443-8956
Web site: http://www.samhsa.gov

Mental Health

American Foundation for Suicide Prevention
120 Wall Street, 22nd Floor
New York, NY 10005
(888) 333-AFSP
(212) 363-3500
Web site: http://www.afsp.org

American Psychological Association
750 First Street NE
Washington, DC 20002-4242
(800) 374-2721
(202) 336-5500
Web site: http://www.apa.org

The Center for Mental Health Services (CMHS)
Knowledge Exchange Network (KEN)
P.O. Box 42490
Washington, DC 20015
(800) 789-2647
Web site: http://www.mentalhealth.org

National Mental Health Association
1021 Prince Street
Alexandria, VA 22314-2971
(703) 684-7722
(800) 969-6642
Web site: http://www.nmha.org

Suicide Awareness/Voices of Education (SA\VE)
7317 Cahill Road, Suite 207
Minneapolis, MN 55424-0507
(800) 784-2483 (hotline)
(952) 946-7998
Web site: http://www.save.org

Suicide Prevention
American Association of Suicidology (AAS)
4201 Connecticut Avenue NW, Suite 408
Washington, DC 20008
(202) 237-2280
Web site: http://www.suicidology.org

Suicide Prevention Advocacy Network (SPANUSA)
5034 Odins Way
Marietta, GA 30068
(888) 649-1366
Web site: http://www.spanusa.org

In Canada

Canadian Centre on Substance Abuse (CCSA)
75 Albert Street, Suite 300
Ottawa, ON K1P 5E7
(613) 235-4048
Web site: http://www.ccsa.ca

Centre for Addiction and Mental Health
33 Russell Street
Toronto, ON M5S 2S1
(416) 535-8501
Web site: http://www.camh.net

Kids Help
439 University Avenue, Suite 300
Toronto, ON M5G 1Y8
(800) 668-6868
(416) 586-5437
Web site: http://kidshelp.sympatico.ca/index.html

For Further Reading

Booher, Dianna Daniels. *Making Friends with Yourself and Other Strangers.* New York: Julian Messner, 1982.

Borysenko, Joan, and Larry Rothstein. *Mending the Body, Minding the Mind.* New York: Bantam Books, 1998.

Casarjian, Robin. *Forgiveness: A Bold Choice for a Peaceful Heart.* New York: Bantam Books, 1992.

Davich, Victor N. *The Best Guide to Meditation.* New York: St. Martin's Press, 1998.

Goleman, Daniel. *The Meditative Mind: The Varieties of Meditative Experience.* New York: St. Martin's Press, 1988.

Harp, David, and Nina Feldman. *The Three Minute Meditator.* 3rd ed. Oakland, CA: New Harbinger Publications, 1996.

Jeffers, Susan. *Feel the Fear and Do It Anyway.* San Diego: Harcourt Brace Jovanovich, 1987.

Kabat-Zinn, Jon. *Wherever You Go, There You Are: Mindfulness Meditation in Everyday Life.* New York: Hyperion, 1994.

Keen, Sam. *Learning to Fly.* New York: Broadway Books, 1999.

Klein, Allen. *The Healing Power of Humor.* Los Angeles: Jeremy P. Tarcher, Inc., 1989.

Kushner, Harold S. *How Good Do We Have to Be? A New Understanding of Guilt and Forgiveness.* Thorndike, ME: G. K. Hall, 1997.

Kwan, Michelle. *The Winning Attitude! What It Takes to Be a Champion.* New York: Hyperion Books for Children, 1999.

LeShan, Lawrence. *How to Meditate: A Guide to Self-Discovery.* Boston, MA: Little, Brown and Company, 1974.

Luks, Allan, and Peggy Payne. *The Healing Power of Doing Good: The Health and Spiritual Benefits of Helping Others.* New York: Fawcett Columbine, 1991.

McCullough, Michael E., Steven J. Sandage, and Everett L. Worthington Jr. *To Forgive Is Human: How to Put Your Past in the Past.* Downers Grove, IL: InterVarsity Press, 1997.

Mortell, Art. *The Courage to Fail.* New York: McGraw-Hill, 1993.

Pennebaker, James W. *Opening Up: The Healing Power of Confiding in Others.* New York: William Morrow and Company, Inc., 1990.

Ruiz, Don Miguel. *The Four Agreements.* San Rafael, CA: Amber-Allen Publishing, Inc., 1997.

Savage, Elayne. *Don't Take It Personally! The Art of Dealing with Rejection.* Oakland, CA: New Harbinger Publications, Inc., 1997.

Telushkin, Joseph. *Words That Hurt, Words That Heal.* New York: William Morrow and Company, Inc., 1996.

Thompson, Gerry M. *Meditation Made Easy.* New York: Sterling Publishing Company, Inc., 1999.

Index

About the Author

Barbara Moe, R.N., M.S.N., and M.S.W., is a nurse, social worker, and writer. She is the author of several books.